First World War
and Army of Occupation
War Diary
France, Belgium and Germany

59 DIVISION
Headquarters, Branches and Services
Royal Army Ordnance Corps
Deputy Assistant Director Ordnance Services
14 February 1917 - 31 July 1919

WO95/3015/1

The Naval & Military Press Ltd
www.nmarchive.com
Published in association with The National Archives

Published by

The Naval & Military Press Ltd

Unit 10 Ridgewood Industrial Park,

Uckfield, East Sussex,

TN22 5QE England

Tel: +44 (0) 1825 749494

www.naval-military-press.com

www.nmarchive.com

This diary has been reprinted in facsimile from the original. Any imperfections are inevitably reproduced and the quality may fall short of modern type and cartographic standards.

Contents

Document type	Place/Title	Date From	Date To
Heading	WO 3015 59th Div D.A. Dir. Ordnance Services 1917 Feb-1919 July		
Heading	59th Division D.A. Dir Ordnance Services Feb 1917-July 1919		
War Diary		14/02/1917	27/03/1917
Heading	War Diary Of D.A.D.O.S. 59th Division From 1st March 1917 To 31 Volume 2		
War Diary		01/03/1917	31/03/1917
Heading	War Diary Of D.A.D.O.S. 59th Division From 1st April 1917 (Volume 3)		
War Diary		01/04/1917	30/04/1917
Miscellaneous	A 59th Division. Appendix 1	24/04/1917	24/04/1917
Heading	War Diary Of D.A.D.O.S. 59th Division From 1st May 1917 To 31st May 1917 (Volume 4)		
War Diary		01/05/1917	31/05/1917
Heading	War Diary Of D.A.D.O.S. 59th Division From 1st June 1917 To June 30th 1917 (Volume IV)		
War Diary		01/06/1917	30/06/1917
Miscellaneous	D.A.D.O.S. 59th Division		
Miscellaneous	Indents		
Miscellaneous	Bulk Stores		
Miscellaneous	Detail Issues		
Miscellaneous	Some Of Principal Items Of Details Issue		
Miscellaneous	Replacement Of Guns, Howitzers And Carriages.		
Miscellaneous	Local purchase		
Miscellaneous	Salvage		
Miscellaneous	Record Of Guns, Howitzers Or Carriages.		
Miscellaneous	Register Of Issues To Officers On Payment		
Miscellaneous	Register Of Orders		
Miscellaneous	List Of Local Purchase The Price Of anyone Description Of Store Recording		
Miscellaneous	D.D.O.S. Fourth Army		
Miscellaneous	Register Of Local Purchase		
Miscellaneous	Records Of Bulk Issues Weekly		
Miscellaneous	Records Of Details Issues 1917		
Miscellaneous	Monthly Establishment Return		
Miscellaneous	A.D.O.S. 111 Crops		
Miscellaneous	D.D.O.S Fourth Army		
Miscellaneous	Records Of The Move Of A Unit		
Miscellaneous	Return Of Corps Area Stores		
Miscellaneous	A Form Messages And Signals.		
Miscellaneous	A form (Messages And Signals)		
Miscellaneous	Order Of Local Purchase		
Miscellaneous	D.A.D.O.S.59th.Division.		
Miscellaneous	D.A.D.O.S. 59th Division No. 03/1266	05/06/1917	05/06/1917
Miscellaneous	Indent For Ordnance Stores	12/06/1917	12/06/1917
Diagram etc	Index Special Bulk		
Miscellaneous	Certified That All Indent Have Been Revised		
Miscellaneous	Rangefinders Infantry		
Miscellaneous	Bulk Book A.B 124		

Miscellaneous	Bulk Wires Book		
Miscellaneous	Dues Out Book A.B 129		
Miscellaneous	2/6 Notts And Derby Regt		
Miscellaneous	Indent For Ordnance Stores	03/05/1917	03/05/1917
Heading	War Diary Of D.A.D.O.S. 59th Division From July 1st 1917 To July 31st 1917 Volume 6		
War Diary		01/07/1917	31/07/1917
Heading	War Diary Of DADOS 59th Division From 1st August 1917 To 31st August 1917		
War Diary		01/08/1917	31/08/1917
Diagram etc	Suggested Plan For Standard Plunge & Shower Bata		
Miscellaneous	D.A.D.O.S., 59th Division.	28/08/1917	28/08/1917
Heading	War Diary Of D.A.D.O.S. 59th Division From Sept 1st 1917 To Sept 30th 1917.		
War Diary		01/09/1917	30/09/1917
Diagram etc	Sketch Plan Of Improvised Machine For Brushing Vermin & From Underclothing		
Heading	?		
Miscellaneous	Copy X.	12/10/1917	12/10/1917
War Diary		01/10/1917	26/10/1917
Heading	War Diary Of D.A.D.O.S. 59th Div. From 1st November 1917 To 30th November 1917 Volume No 10		
War Diary		01/11/1917	30/11/1917
Heading	War Diary Of D.A.D.O.S. 59th Div. From 1st Dec. 1917 To 31st Dec. 1917 Volume 10		
War Diary		01/12/1917	31/01/1918
Heading	War Diary Of D.A.D.O.S. 59th Div. From 1st Feb 1918 To 28th Feb 1918 Volume No 13		
War Diary		01/02/1918	28/03/1918
Miscellaneous	A.D.O.S. VIth Corps. Sheet No.2	30/03/1918	30/03/1918
Miscellaneous	D.A.D.O.S. 59th Division	27/03/1918	27/03/1918
Heading	War Diary Of D.A.D.O.S. 59th Divn. From 1st April 1918 To 30th April 1918 Volume No 18		
War Diary		01/04/1918	30/04/1918
Heading	War Diary Of D.A.D.O.S. 59 Div From 1st May 1918 31st May 1918 Volume No 16.		
War Diary		01/05/1918	31/07/1918
Heading	War Diary Of DADOS 59th Division From 1st Aug 1918 To 31st Aug 1918 Volume No 19		
War Diary		01/08/1918	31/08/1918
Heading	War Diary Of D.A.D.O.S. 59th Division From 1st Sept 1918 To 30th Sept 1918 Volume 20		
War Diary		01/09/1918	30/09/1918
Heading	War Diary Of D.A.D.O.S. 59 Division From 1st October 1918 To 31st October 1918. Volume No-22		
War Diary		01/10/1918	31/10/1918
Miscellaneous	H.q. 59 Division	16/01/1919	16/01/1919
War Diary		01/02/1919	28/02/1919
War Diary	Verquin	01/03/1919	07/03/1919
War Diary	Beaumarais	08/03/1919	30/04/1919
War Diary	Beaumarais	01/05/1919	26/06/1919
War Diary	Beaumarais France	01/07/1919	31/07/1919

WO 3015

59th Div

D. A. Dir. ORDNANCE
SERVICES

1917 Feb –
1919 July

59TH DIVISION

D.A.DIR ORDNANCE SERVICES ✓

FEB 1917 - ~~DEC 1918~~

JULY 1919

Instructions regarding War Diaries and Intelligence Summaries are contained in F. S. Regs., Part II. and the Staff Manual respectively. Title pages will be prepared in manuscript.

WAR DIARY
~~or~~
~~INTELLIGENCE SUMMARY.~~

(Erase heading not required.)

Army Form C. 2118.

D.A.D.O.S.
59th Division. Feb 1917

Vol 1

Place	Date 1917.	Hour	Summary of Events and Information	Remarks and references to Appendices
	14/2		Arrived BOULOGNE.	
	15/2		" VILLERS BRETONNEUX (H.Q.111.Corps) (62 D.O.29. C.O.)	
	16/2 to 22/2		Arranged for Sundry Stores in advance of arrival of troops. Discussed matters with A.D.O.S.111.Corps & visited D.A.Ds.O.S. of 1st. 48th. & 50th.Divisions. Went with A.D.O.S.111.Corps to call on D.D.O.S. 4th. Army.	
	23/2		Opened Store at SALEUX (AMIENS 17.2.D.)	
	24/2		Routine.	
	25/2		" Went to A.D.O.S.111.Corps conference of D.A.Ds.O.S.	
	26/2		"	
	27/2		Opened Store at BAYONVILLERS (62D. W.2.A.)	
	28/2		Closed Store at SALEUX (AMIENS 17.2.D.) and opened office at BAYONVILLERS.(62.D.W2.A)	
	1/3		Routine.	
	2/3		do.	
	3/3		do.	
	4/3		do. Went to A.D.O.S.111 Corps conference.	
	5/3		do.	
	6/3		do.	
	7/3		do.	
	8/3		Moved Stores to PROYART (62D-R20-B)	
	9/3		" my Billet to PROYART.	
	10/3		Routine. Men reported for opening of Divisional Workshops.	
	11-26/3		Routine.	
	27/3		Visited all Staff Captains.	

J Dodds Capt
D.A.D.O.S.
59th Divn

A5834 Wt. W4973 M687 750,000 8/16 D. D. & L. Ltd. Forms/C.2118/13.

Vol II

Confidential

War Diary

of

D.A.D.O.S. 59th Divn

From 1st March 1917 To 31

(Volume 2)

Instructions regarding War Diaries and Intelligence Summaries are contained in F. S. Regs., Part II. and the Staff Manual respectively. Title pages will be prepared in manuscript.

WAR DIARY

~~or~~

~~INTELLIGENCE SUMMARY.~~

(Erase heading not required.)

Army Form C. 2118.

Place	Date	Hour	Summary of Events and Information	Remarks and references to Appendices
	1917			
	1/3 to 3/3		Routine.	
	4/3		do. Went to A.D.O.S. Conference.	
	5/3 to 7/3		do.	
	8/3		Moved stores to PROYART (62D-R20-B)	
	9/3		" my Billet to PROYART.	
	10/3		Routine. Men reported for opening of Divisional Workshops.	
	11/3 to 26/3		Routine.	
	27/3		Visited all Staff Captains.	
	28/3 to 30/3		Routine.	
	31/3		Railhead changed to SATYRE. (M23-D-08)	

J Dodds Capt
D.A.D.O.S.
59th Divn

A5834 Wt. W4973 M687 750,000 8/16 D. D. & L. Ltd. Forms/C.2118/13.

Vol 3

<u>Confidential</u>

War Diary

of

D.A.D.O.S 59th Division

From 1st April 1917. To 30th April 1917

(Volume 3)

Instructions regarding War Diaries and Intelligence Summaries are contained in F. S. Regs., Part II. and the Staff Manual respectively. Title pages will be prepared in manuscript.

WAR DIARY

~~or~~

~~INTELLIGENCE SUMMARY.~~

(Erase heading not required.)

Army Form C. 2118.

Place	Date	Hour	Summary of Events and Information	Remarks and references to Appendices
	April			
	1		Attended Conference of A.D.O.S. 111 Corps.	
	2 to 5		Routine.	
	6		A.D.O.S. 111 Corps called and inspected Office, Stores & Armourers' Workshop	
	7		Routine.	
	8		Attended Conference of A.D.O.S. 111 Corps.	
	9		Stores moved to Estrees-en-Chaussee.	
	10 to 12		Routine.	
	13		A.D.O.S. 111 Corps called and inspected Office and Stores. Moved Office and Billets under canvas.	
	14, 15		Routine.	
	16		Visited all Staff Captains.	
	17 to 19		Routine.	
	20		Capt. G.G.Bannermen, 4th B'n "Queens" (RWS) Regt, attached, arrived.	
	21		.. .. left to join 42nd Div'n.	
	22		Attended Conference of A.D.O.S. 111 Corps.	
	23		Routine.	
	24		Visited all Staff Captains. Report on Ordnance services during Advance sent Hqrs, 59th Division, (copy attached)	Appendix 1.
	25 & 26		Routine.	
	27		A.D.O.S. called.	
	28		Visited all Staff Captains.	
	29		Attended Conference of A.D.O.S. 111 Corps.	
	30		Routine.	

[illegible] Capt
D.A.D.O.S.
59th Div'n

APPENDIX 1.

Copy.

"A"

59th Division.

ORDNANCE.

To commence with, Ordnance Stores were taken from my Store at Proyart to refilling point at Estrees. As soon as it was possible to take the lorries over the roads, a forward dump was opened at Pruisle, (30th March), and units drew from there at any hour which suited them. On the 9th April the Store was moved forward to Estrees-en-Chaussee and the dump closed. On the units pushing forward, stores were taken for all units in the Roisel district to that point by lorry and handed over. As a number of Q.M's stores were there this saved the Transport a great deal. The arrangement is still being carried out.

All stores indented for and received from the Base were got to the units, and there were no complaints. Everything ran as smoothly as could be expected including the delivery of a large quantity of tentage.

(signed) J. Dodds. Capt.

24-4-17. D.A.D.O.S. 59th Division.

Confidential

Vol 4

War Diary

of

D.A.D.O.S. 59th Division

From 1st May 1917.

To 31st May 1917.

(Volume 4)

Army Form C. 2118.

WAR DIARY
or
INTELLIGENCE SUMMARY.
(*Erase heading not required.*)

Instructions regarding War Diaries and Intelligence Summaries are contained in F. S. Regs., Part II. and the Staff Manual respectively. Title pages will be prepared in manuscript.

Place	Date	Hour	Summary of Events and Information	Remarks and references to Appendices
	1917 May			
	1-2		Routine.	
	3		Visited all Staff Captains.	
	4-5		Routine.	
	6		Attended Conference A.D.O.S. Office, 111 Corps.	
	7-12		Routine.	
	13		A.D.O.S. 111 Corps called.	
	14		Routine.	
	15		1 Truck Blankets & General Stores returned to Base.	
	16		2 do. do. do.	
	17		Visited all Staff Captains.	
	18-19		Routine.	
	20		1 Truck Gum Boots & Capes Mackintosh returned to Base.	
	21		1 do Sundry Winter Stores returned to Base.	
	22		Routine.	
	23		2 Trucks Blankets returned to Base.	
	23-24		Called on A.D.O.S. XV Corps.	
	24		Site for Stores & Office selected at Equancourt. (Map ref. 57c.V10.D.Cen.)	
			1 Truck Sundry Winter Stores returned to Base.	
	25		2 Trucks Gum Boots & Capes Mackintosh returned to Base.	
	26		2 do. do. do.	
			Came into XV Corps.	
			Site for Stores & Office at Equancourt cancelled, & fresh site selected by A.A.& Q.M.G. near Ytres station, (Map ref. 57c. P32 Cen.)	
	26-27		Moved Stores to Ytres.	
	27		2 Trucks Blankets returned to Base	
	28		Moved Office to Ytres.	
	29		1 Truck Gum Boots & Capes Mackintosh returned to Base.	
	30-31		Routine.	

S Dodds
Capt
D.A.D.O.S.
59th Div

Vol 5

CONFIDENTIAL

WAR DIARY

OF

D.A.D.O.S. 59th DIVISION

FROM. 1st JUNE, 1917. (VOLUME IV) TO JUNE 30th 1917.

Army Form C. 2118.

WAR DIARY
or
INTELLIGENCE SUMMARY.
(Erase heading not required.)

Instructions regarding War Diaries and Intelligence Summaries are contained in F. S. Regs., Part II. and the Staff Manual respectively. Title pages will be prepared in manuscript.

Place	Date	Hour	Summary of Events and Information	Remarks and references to Appendices
	1917. June 1/6		Routine. No. 014032 Sub-Conductor A.Kerry A.O.C., B.W.O. 177th. Infantry Brigade, Evacuated 26-5-17.	
	2.		Routine.	
	3.		Attended Conference, A.D.O.S. Office, 111. Corps.	
	4 to 7.		Routine. Memoranda on organisation and system, to A.D.O.S. 111. Corps, (Copies of all his and my Memoranda &c. attached)	No. "1"
	8.		Visited all Staff Captains.	
	9.		do. do.	
	10.		Balance of Winter Clothing withdrawn (2nd.Blankets)	
	"		Attended Conference, A.D.O.S. Office, 111 Corps.	
	11 & 12.		Routine.	
	13.		Visited all Staff Captains.	
	14.		1 Truck Blankets returned to Base.	
	15.		Routine.	
	16.		"	
	17.		Attended Conference, A.D.O.S. Office, 111. Corps.	
	"		1 Truck Blankets returned to Base.	
	18.		Routine.	
	19.		Capt. Dodds, DADOS. proceeded to England on leave.	
	20.		Balance of Blankets returned to Base.	
	21 to 23.		Routine.	
	24.		Conference, A.D.O.S. Office 111.Corps, attended by Chief Clerk.	
	25.		Routine.	
	26.		A.D.O.S. 111.Corps called and inspected Store etc.	
	27.		Visited all Staff Captains.	
	28.		Routine.	
	29.		Capt.Dodds, DADOS. returned off leave.	
	30.		Routine. A.D.O.S. 111. Corps called.	

S Dodds Capt
D.A.D.O.S.
59th Div

A5834 Wt. W4973/M687 750,000 8/16 D. D. & L. Ltd. Forms/C.2118/13.

201

(Copy) A.D.O.S. 111. Corps.
No.14/107a

D.A.D.O.S.
59th. Division.

Your attention is drawn to S.S.358. "Instructions to Ordnance Officers in the Field". Every W.O. and clerk should be in possession of a copy amended to date. The following books should also be in your Office:-

Fourth Army Standing Orders.
Extracts from G.R.Os. parts 1 & 11 dated 1-1-17.
S.S.360 Notes on Transport, Ordnance, Supply and Requisitioning Services.
G.1098 for all Units of the Division.
Priced Vocabulary of Stores.

2. Various instructions on the subject of accounting are attached. These are to be carefully studied and compared with the system employed by you, the pros and cons considered and result reported to me. The system employed must ensure that the information required is available in your office.

3. The "pro formas" for telegraphic indents and for returns must be carefully followed, and returns are to be rendered up to date.

4. I want to see you at my office at 11 a.m. every Sunday.

5. The following Divisional Reserves are to be maintained.-

Small Box Respirators.	1000
Spare Boxes. (Authy. A.R.O.698)	1500 x
P.H.Helmets. (Authy.Q.M.G., Q.O.S.317/39/A d/7/10/16)	2500
Goggles Spicer Pattern. (Authy.Q.M.G. Q.O.S.317/4/A d/-20/4/16)	700
Springs Inner, 18 Pr.	36
Springs Outer. 18 Pr.	36

x Tool for detaching container 1 per Coy. of Infantry and other Units of corresponding strength (on charge of Gas N.C.O.)

6. All changes of position of D.H.Q., Offices and Dumps of D.A.D.O.S. and Divisional Salvage Officer should be reported by D.R.L.S. to this office.

7. Attention is drawn to S.S. 358 para 21. D.A.Ds.O.S. must obtain early information as to the formation to which a Unit or Units is moving. Pro forma for report is attached "L".

8. A return of Corps and Area Stores held by your Division will be forwarded to reach this office on Saturdays. (pro forma attached) "M" Any of these stores not required by the Division, should be returned to Ordnance Corps Stores, due notice being given.

9. Whenever your Division takes or hands over Trench Stores, the number of such stores transferred will be reported to this office. For list of trench stores see A.S.O.83.

H.Q.,111.Corps. (Sd) S.C.Lewis. Major.
A.D.O.S.

INDENTS.

All indents from Units will be given a consecutive number (S.S.358 para.6) and the following details registered in a book (129) kept for the purpose. See pro forma "C"

When receipts of indents are acknowledged by Base the entry against them should be ticked off.

Indents for stores in excess of authorised issues should be supported by approval of G.O.C., Division before being referred to Corps Hd.Qrs. (S.S.358 para.18)

Indents for clothing and necessaries to replace other unserviceable through wilfulness or neglect should be similarly endorsed " To replace others unserviceable and charged for" S.S.358 para. 16. G.R.O.1865.

Indents for clothing and necessaries for free issues should bear certificate of O.C.,Unit to the effect that the articles are required "To replace others unserviceable by fair wear and tear.

Indents for vehicles- S.S.358 para.18 and 20, S.S.360 page 9.

Indents for M.T. Units- S.S. 358 para. 19.

Indents for issues on replacement to Officers- S.S.358 para. 46 G.R.O.326. These indents are entered also in separate register See pro forma "B"

Indents for guns,(including Machine Guns) Howitzers and Carriages are dealt with on a separate sheet.

Correspondence on indents to be attached to the indent. In the case of hasteners the indent should be endorsed "Hastened (date)" only.

In the case of a ~~special~~ first supply specially authorised, the authority should be entered in remarks column of Register of Indents and sufficient lines left to allow of units indents to be entered as they come in. One consolidated indent is sent to the Base for all the Units affected.

Incomplete indents and completed indents of Units should be kept in separate files by Units.

Incompleted indents will be reviewed every fortnight when the report on stores due out is received from the Base. (S.S.358 para.14) The Base should be informed of any indents or items that may be cancelled. (S.S. 358. para. 8)

BULK STORES.

Three lines are added to Bulk Issue Form above Total line and are worded Received, Issued, and Stock (date), respectively.

Indents checked and if approved entered straight into Brigade Bulk Issue Form, a separate form being kept for each Brigade and for Divisional Troops.

On proper day - telegram made out in office and despatched by 4 P.M.

Totals for each Brigade and for Divisional Troops are entered on consolidated Bulk Issue Form. Brigade Bulk Issue Forms are then sent to Brigade W.Os. and Foreman of Divisional Troops at dump.

When stores are received, distribution is first made from consolidated Bulk Issue Form. Brigade W.Os. and Foremen enter up totals received and distribute according to the entries on Brigade Bulk Issue Forms.

Demands for small quantities should be met in full, any shortage in the numbers received from the Base being adjusted by not issuing larger quantities in full.

Put one line through figure to be amended and write altered figure immediately above it.

Signatures for issues should be obtained in A.B. 108.

As stores are issued, the corresponding figures on Brigade Bulk Issue Form are circled and the Form is sent to Office on day before next bulk telegram is prepared.

1. Total of circled entries gives Issues.
2. Total of circled entries and plain entries gives receipts.
3. Total of plain entries gives stock.
4. Total of plain entries and differencies between crossed out figures and the figures immediately above it gives Dues Out.

Office carry forward stock and any demands not met to next bulk issue forms and mark up total issues, receipts and stocks on consolidated Bulk Issue Form.

RECORD OF BULK ISSUES.

Brigade W.Os. and Foremen Divisional Troops will keep a bulk issue book, a separate page for each item and ruled as pro forma "G". The totals issued to each unit for the week will be entered.

The final column gives total issued to the Brigade.

This total should agree with the total for the Brigade entered by the office in the consolidated Bulk Issue Form.

DETAIL ISSUES.

S.S. 360 page 17.

Record will be kept of the principal items of detail issue. A list of some of these is attached, but the D.A.D.O.S. will add to them as necessary.

A page will be allotted to each item, a separate book for each Brigade and Divisional Troops.

As soon as indent is approved, the date of the indent and number of the item will be entered in pencil against the unit-pro forma "H" attached.

When item is received, the entry will be made in ink.

When item is issued the entry will have a circle drawn round it.

If number demanded is not all received, balance still due will be entered in pencil on a fresh line but with original date.

If numbers received are not all issued, cross out original receipt figure and enter in ink above it number remaining to be issued, at the same time making a circled entry with the original date, on a fresh line.

1. Total of pencil entries gives dues from Base.
2. Total of ink entries not circled or crossed out gives stock.
3. Total of pencil entries and ink entries not circled or crossed out gives dues out to units.
4. Total of circled entries gives issues.

2 plus 4 gives receipts from Base.

Some of the principal items of detail issue.

Bayonets.

Bicycles.

Binoculars.

Cable, Electric.

Clinometers.

Compasses.

Directors,

Harness, Sets.

Helios.

Lamps Electric.

Lamps Signalling. B.

Periscopes.

Pistols.

Rangefinders.

Rifles.

Saddlery, Sets.

Sights.

Stretchers.

Telephones.

Telescopes.

Tools, Sets.

Watches.

Wheels.

Poles, Draught.

Guns,

Vehicles.

All 1st. Issues as they occur.

REPLACEMENT
OF
GUNS, HOWITZERS & CARRIAGES.

Indents for Guns, (including Machine Guns) Howitzers or Carriages. S.S.358 para. 11 as amended by D.O. 438, and circular O.S.A. 1/139 dated 16/4/17. G.R.O.1199.

These indents are also entered in separate register, see pro forma "A"

Form of telegraphic indent for these stores is attached. This should be carefully followed. (See also S.S.358 para. 10)

Within 7 days of condemnation, the return to Railhead of the condemned Gun, Howitzer or Carriage will be reported by wire to D.D.O.S. Army and repeated to A.D.O.S.,Corps. Following information will be given:

(a) Original indent wire number and name of Unit concerned.

(b) Registered number of Gun, Howitzer or Carriage.

(c) Railhead to which sent.

(d) Date.

(e) Truck number.

Form of wire is attached.

Until Gun, Howitzer or Carriage is returned to Railhead a report will be sent every seventh day by D.R.L.S. to D.D.O.S., Army and A.D.O.S., Corps giving reason for delay.

In cases where the Gun, Howitzer or Carriage is destroyed to such an extent that it is not possible to return it to Railhead, the first report will say so and be sufficient.

Receipt of Gun, Howitzer or Carriage in replacement will be reported by wire to D.D.O.S., Army and repeated to A.D.O.S., Corps.

Form of wire is attached.

LOCAL PURCHASE.

see S.S.358 para 47 (as amended by D.O.318) -63. S.S.360 pages 16 & 17.- G.R.Os. 12, 439, 880, 683. A.S.Os. 52, 56,57. D.O.S. circular O.S.A.1/6913. Field Service Regulations part 11. page 44 para.4.

Textile Stores are not to be purchased in France- A.R.O.1009.

Amount.	Authority.	Remarks.
Up to £5.	D.A.D.O.S.	
£5 to £25.	G.O.C.,Divn. in writing.	Weekly list to A.D.O.S. pro forma attached "D"
£25 to£100	In case of urgency G.O.C. Divn. in writing.	Covering Authority of D.D.O.S. necessary. pro forma attached "E"
Over £100	D.O.S.	Authority obtained before purchase thro' D.D.O.S. Pro forma attached "E" In case of urgency request giving full details may be sent by wire.

A weekly return of all purchases of whatever value will be forwarded to reach A.D.O.S., 111. Corps every Saturday, on A.F.W. 3336. Copy of form attached. This return will include purchases made by other Officers but passed as correct by D.A.D.O.S.

A register of all Local Purchases will be kept- pro forma "F" attached.

The case of a purchase by an Officer, other than an A.O.D. Officer, is dealt with in A.S.O.57. The transaction is not correct until the authority necessary for the particular amount involved has been obtained.

SALVAGE.

A.S.O. 97 (c). S.S.358 paras. 2 (7) & 37 -45.
S.S. 360 pages 19-23.

1. You should keep in constant touch with Divisional Salvage Officers and visit periodically the Divisional Salvage Dumps.

2. Ensure that stores at Salvage Dumps are disposed of without undue delay either (a) by removal by various services concerned for re-issue or repair, (b) by return to Railhead for despatch to the Base, (c) by destruction if neither they nor any portions of them can be disposed of as produce.

3. Ensure that demands on the Base are decreased in proportion to the recovery of stores by Salvage.

4. Report, after enquiry, any unusually large amount of stores salved in a serviceable condition.

5. Keep a record of all stores received from Salvage or sources other than the Base or Local Purchase, with a note as to method of disposal, e.g.

Bulk issues weeks ending 7 & 14.2.18.
Indent No................."A" Regt.

Every effort must be made to utilize the lorries allotted to you to the full, both when coming and going.

By careful coordination with the Divisional Salvage Officer it should be possible to give him all the assistance he requires to move his salved stores to Railhead.

"A"

RECORD OF GUNS, HOWITZERS OR CARRIAGES.

Formation.	Unit.	Indent No.	Date.	GUN OR HOWITZER.			CARRIAGE.		Date of Receipt from Base.	RETURN TO BASE.		
				Reg: No.	Reasons of condemnation & remarks.	With or without fittings.	Reg: No.	Reasons of condemnation & remarks.		Name of Railhead.	Date handed in at Railhead	Truck No.

A separate page or 2 pages for each nature of Gun or Howitzer.

"B"

REGISTER OF ISSUES TO OFFICERS ON PAYMENT.

Indent No.	Date.	Rank.	Name & Initials.	I.V. No.	Items Issued.	Price.	No. of A.F.W. 3226.	Date sent to P.M.	Date rec'd by P.M.

"C"

REGISTER OF INDENTS.

Name of Unit.	Units Indent No.	Date of Indent.	Ordnance No.	Date rec'd by Ordce.	Date sent to Base.	Remarks and if hastened the date.

D.

List of Local Purchases the price of any one description of store exceeding £5 but not exceeding £25.

C.O. No.	Date	Description of Stores	No. ordered	Rate Rs.	Rate Cts	Amount Rs.	Amount Cts	Service for which required	Sanctioned Account

The above purchases are considered necessary and are authorized

O.A.O.S. Division

1907

G.O.C. Division

"E"

L.P.O., No. _______________

D.D.O.S.
Fourth Army.

Authority is requested for the purchase of stores as detailed below, the price of any one description of stores

{ exceeding £25 but not exceeding £100.
{ exceeding £100.

Nature of Store.	No.	Rate		Amount.		Service for which required.
		Fcs.	Cts.	Fcs.	Cts.	

The above purchase is considered necessary.

Date_____________ G.O.C., Division.

Date_____________ D.A.D.O.S., Division.

Register of Local Purchases

F

P. O. No.	Order of Indent No.	Order of Indent Date	Description of Stores	Number or Quantity	Rate \$	Rate Cts.	Amount \$	Amount Cts.	Name of Contractor	Authy. for Purchase and Date	Remarks and Statement as to Imprest Account through which paid

"G"

RECORD OF BULK ISSUES. WEEKLY.

Boots.

Date.	"A" Regt.	"B" Regt.							Total.
12-5-16									
19-5-16									
26-5-16									

"H"

Record of Detail Issues 1917.

BICYCLES.

"A" Rgt.		"B" Rgt.		"C" Rgt.		"D" Rgt.							
Date	No.	Date	No.	Date	No.	Date	No.	Date	No.	Date	No.	Date	No.
22/8	4	24/8	4	23/8	2	22/8	2						
				23/8	2	22/8	2						

Dues from Base.	6
Stock	2
Dues out to Units	8
Issues.	8

"I"

MONTHLY ESTABLISHMENT RETURN.

CORPS/ ____________ FOURTH ARMY.

DIVISION. ____________

D.A.D.O.S. ____________

OTHER OFFICERS. ____________ DATE. ____________

Regtl. No.	Permt. Rank.	Acting Rank.	Name.	Trade or calling.	Remarks.

DIVISIONAL HEADQUARTERS

-- INFANTRY BRIGADE

-- INFANTRY BRIGADE

-- INFANTRY BRIGADE

"J"

A.D.O.S.
111. Corps.

The following is a statement of bulk issues for months of __________ to the ____Division.

Nomenclature.				Totals	Nomenclature				Totals
Boots Ankle prs.					Pegs Picktg.				
Shirts.					Posts Picket.				
Socks, prs.					Ropes Head.				
Drawers,cotn.					Reins.				
Dressings Fld.					Ropes Heel.				
Oil Lub.G.S.					Ropes Picketg.				
Mineral Jelly.					Mallets,Heal peg.				
Dubbin.					Tools Intr.				
Grease Lub.					Camp Kettles.				
Soap,Yellow.					Blankets G.S.				
Soap Soft.					Sheets Grnd.				
Shoes,Horse.					Cloths Sponge.				
" Mule.					Cotton Waste.				
Gt.Coats.					Flannelette.				
Jackets S.D.					Haversacks.				
Trousers S.D.					Waterbottles.				
Pantaloons,prs.					Mess Tins.				
Puttees,prs.					Pullthro's Wts.				
Drawers Wooln.					" Cords.				
Vests.					" Gauzes.				
Smoke Helmets.					" Compte.				
					Bags Nose.				
					Nets Hay.				

D.A.D.O.S.

"K"

TENTAGE RETURN

MONTH ENDING ____________

FORMATION.	TENTS															TARPAULINS & SAIL COVERS *			COVERS TRENCH			TENT BOTTOMS SETS		
	CSL			SHELTER			STORE			OPERATING			MARQUEE											
	In use	Not in use	Due from Base	In use	Not in use	Due from Base	In use	Not in use	Due from Base	In use	Not in use	Due from Base	In use	Not in use	Due from Base	In use	Not in use	Due from Base	In use	Not in use	Due from Base	In use	Not in use	Due from Base

* Sail covers to be shown separately

"L"

Record of the move of a unit.

SECRET

D.R.L.S.

O.O., Base or Bases if more than one is affected.
Ordnance Officer of the Formation to which Unit is going.
D.D.O.S., Fourth Army.
A.D.O.S., 111. Corps.

MOVE.

(Unit or portion of Unit) ____ from ____ Division.

to ________ Division. or Corps Troops.

Addressed to Bases or Base.

Repeated O.O., of Formation
D.D.O.S., Fourth Army.
A.D.O.S., 111Corps.

Date.

D.A.D.O.S., ____ Division.

"M"

RETURN OF CORPS AREA STORES.

______Division.

Week ending__________

Item	Number with troops.	Number with DADOS	Remarks.
Boots, Gum Thigh.			
Braziers.			
Capes Mackintosh.			
Camp Kettles.			
Chaff cutting M/cs.			
"Clayton" Disinfectors,			
Extra Saddles.			
Fire Extinguishers.			
Hot Food Containers.			
Huts.			
Lamps, Hurricane.			
Ladders, Observation.			
Lamps Sig. "French" Elec.			
Latrine Buckets.			
Marquees.			
Matrasses.			
Mats, Traversor.			
Packsaddlery Sets.			
Pack Carriers, 18-pdr.			
" " 4.5.Howr.			
Periscopes No.9.			
Pistols Very 1"			
Revolvers.			
Shower Baths.			
Soyers Stoves.			
Snow Ploughs.			
Stoves for Amm.Dumps.			
Strombos Horns.			
Tarpaulins 30 X 20.			
" 30 X 30.			
Telescopes S.1.			
" S.2.			
Tents C.S L.			
" Shelter.			
" Store.			
Trench Covers.			
" Boards. Sets.			
Tip Carts.			
Tubs Washing.			

D.A.D.O.S., Division.

"A" Form.

MESSAGES AND SIGNALS.

Army Form C. 2121.
(In pads of 100.)

No. of Message..............

Prefix............ Code.............. m. | Words. | Charge.

Office of Origin and Service Instructions.

Sent
At..............m.
To..............
By..............

This message is on a/c of:
.... *Service.*

" PRO FORMA "
(Signature of "Franking Officer.")

Recd. at .... m.
Date..............
From..............
By..............

TO { Ordnance, Havre.

Sender's Number.	Day of Month.	In reply to Number.	AAA
* X. 100/4	[illegible]/5/17		

Indent AAA			
110	Siege	Battery	(in code)
AAA 6"	26 cwt.	Howitzer and	Carriage
(in code)	[illegible] one	AAA [illegible]	[illegible]
and	Sights	AAA	[illegible]
2971	[illegible] and	1264	AAA
Shell	[illegible]	AAA	
Addressed	Ordnance	Havre.	repeated
G.H.Q.	D. Ord.	4th. Army	(in code)
III Corps	(in code)		

From Ordnance

Place 1[illegible]0 Division (in code)

Time

The above may be forwarded as now corrected. (Z)

X. No. of Division [illegible]

Censor. Signature of Addressor or person authorised to telegraph in his name.

* This line should be erased if not required.

(3198.) Wt. W 12952/M1294. 375,000 Pads. 1/17. H. W. & V., Ld. (E. 818.)

"A" Form.

Army Form C. 2121.
(In pads of 100.)

MESSAGES AND SIGNALS.

No. of Message..............

Prefix............Code.............. m | Words. | Charge.

Office of Origin and Service Instructions.

Sent
At..............m.
To..............
By..............

This message is on a/c of:

.... *Service.*

(Signature of "Franking Officer.")

Recd. at .... m.
Date..............
From ....
By..............

TO Ordnance 4th. Army.

Sender's Number.	Day of Month.	In reply to Number.	AAA
* 100/83	29/5/17		

Received	6" 26 cwt	Howitzer	(in code)
2983 and	Carriage	1896	off
indent	100 over	4	dated
22 AAA	Addressed	Ordnance	4th. Army
repeated	Ordnance	3rd. Corps.	(in code)
I.O.M.	20 Ordnance	Workshop.	

From Ordnance 100 Division (in code)
Place
Time

The above may be forwarded as now corrected. (Z)

Censor. Signature of Addressor or person authorised to telegraph in his name.

* This line should be erased if not required.

(3198.) Wt. W 12952/M1294. 375,000 Pads. 1/17. H. W. & V., Ld. (E. 818.)

"A" Form.

Army Form C. 2121.
(In pads of 100.)

MESSAGES AND SIGNALS.

No. of Message..............

Prefix.......... Code.......... m	Words.	Charge.	This message is on a/c of:	Recd. at .... m.
Office of Origin and Service Instructions.	Sent		.... Service.	Date..............
......A..............................	At..............m.			From ....
....	To..................			
....	By..................		(Signature of "Franking Officer.")	By..................

TO { Ordnance 4th. Army.

Sender's Number.	Day of Month.	In reply to Number.	AAA
* 100/73	26/5/17		

Lr	100	over	4
dated	22 AAA		
110	Siege	Battery	(in code)
AAA	2871	and	1384
from	Railhead	(in code)	dated
26	in	truck	17062 AAA

Addressed Ordnance 4th. Army repeated Ordnance III Corps. (in code)

From Ordnance, 100 Division. (in code)
Place
Time

The above may be forwarded as now corrected.

(Z)

Censor. | Signature of Addressor or person authorised to telegraph in his name.

* This line should be erased if not required.

(3198.) Wt. W 12952/M1294. 375,000 Pads. 1/17. H. W. & V., Ld. (E. 818.)

Return of Local Purchase Orders (A3W 3531)

Headquarters week ending ____________

Total expenditure on bills passed for payment during week ended ____________ = ____________ Francs ____________ Centimes

Army Ordnance Depot ____________

Local Purchase Order		Description of Stores	No. or Qty.	Rate		Amount		Authority
No.	Date			Frs.	Cents	Frs.	Cents	
			Total					

(Copy)

D.A.D.O.S.59th.Division.
No. 03/1266.

A.D.O.S.
111.Corps.

I have looked over and considered your 14/107a. The principle underlying your memorandum and that employed in this office and store is practically the same but differs somewhat in detail. Nearly every D.A.D.O.S. feels certain that his system is much better than any other in use at the Front and S.S.358 gives him a wide discretion. Many A.Ds.O.S. have schemes which they have tried or seen tried and which they would like to see put in operation by all D.A.Ds. O.S. but the constant change of Divisions from Corps to Corps makes this impossible.

I have dealt with your memorandum according to the numbers of your paras leaving No.2, the most important, to be dealt with in a separate minute which I am preparing. My criticism is a frank expression of opinion, which I presume is what you require.

(1) This is in order now.

(2) The "pro formas" for telegraphic indents have been amended to read at the foot "not in code"

The method used to ensure "Returns" being sent on the proper day is by drawing up a monthly calendar which is kept on the Chief Clerk's desk, and marking the day any return is due to be sent off.

In the XV, and Cavalry Corps, no Corps and Area Return is called for. The figures shown in the return cannot be correct and it would therefore appear to me to be a waste of time rendering it, except when a Division takes over a new area.

Another return not called for in the two Corps I have mentioned is "Stock at Divisional Dumps". There is very little change in this from week to week. It consists of the gas Appliance reserves and very little else of any account. I always show the Divisional Laundry working stock, but it is not held at an Ordnance Dump. It went into the Return when the Laundry started (I held the initial stock) and has remained there ever since. Could this Return be done away with and so further reduce the paper work, which is pretty heavy as it is?

A Tentage Return is rendered by me to you and to Corps "Q" by my "Q". Would it be possible to cancel the one sent by me to you?. The information has to be obtained through "Q" who could perhaps send his Return to Corps "Q" in duplicate, if necessary, and so reduce work.

(3) The Certificate re indents is given by me on the attached form marked "A"B Those outstanding are not of necessity cancelled, but the stores are usually hastened.

(4) Noted.

Continued.

(5) Noted, but I am of the opinion that the D.A.C. Establishment of Springs Running Out, is better held by the I.O.M. for the reasons given by me at the last conference.

(6) Noted.

(7) Noted. I have requested "Q" to keep me informed of movements as early as possible.

(8) Dealt with under para 3, Second half of para noted.

(9) "Q" has been requested to supply the information.

(Sd) J.DODDS.

Capt.

4-6-17 D.A.D.O.S.,59th. Division.

D.A.D.O.S., 59th. Division.
No. 03/1266.

A.D.O.S.
111. Corps.

I have drawn up the following notes with reference to your 14/107a, which I hope will be useful.

INDENTS.

Only "detail indents" are registered and numbered as laid down. No useful purpose would be served by registration of Bulk Indents as full particulars are noted in the Bulk Demands Books. Very few Divisions, if any, register Bulk Indents. We tried the system, but found that it took one man nearly all his time dealing with the matter. S.S. 358 para. 7, outlines the reason for numbering them, i.e. so that they can be referred to in correspondence and telegrams with the Base. There is no correspondence with the Base on Bulk Indents.

Instead of the wording "To replace unserviceable and charged for" we make the Unit write on the indent the words "on payment".

"First Supplies" are not registered by me in the way you mention. A.F.G. 994 (in a book of 150 forms) is kept for the purpose of demanding Special Bulk issues. One copy which shows how distribution is to be made is left in the book, which is indexed on the inside of the cover. This does away with the handling and registration of a lot of indents and gives a perfect record of all Special Bulk Demands and Issues. The saving in Indent Forms must also be considerable. A specimen page marked "A" is attached and on the back thereof an example of the index is given.

We have not been in the habit of "P.A" completed indents in separate pads by Units. They are rarely referred to and can be found if required quite easily. We can do this however if you so wish.

Incompleted indents are reviewed constantly and each month the attached, marked "B" is signed by the B.W.O. & Quartermaster or Q.M.S. This certificate is fastened into the"Incomple Indents" pads.

BULK, DETAIL and UNSERVICEABLE.

I do not agree with the use of loose forms for Bulk work in the Field. Work has to be carried out at times in Lorries and in Tents, and loose forms are liable to be blown about and spoiled by rain. As briefly as possible I will explain our system, but before doing so would point out that the system outlined by you for detail issues is practically keeping a progressive ledger. All we keep is a record of principal detail issues, as laid down in S.S.358, para.2 (see "C" attached). There should be no stock of "detail stores". You do not take up the question of "U" stores, but I have done so as I think it an important part of a D.A.Ds.O.S. work. Unless something of the kind is done, there can be no efficient check on the demands of Units, at least, that is my opinion.

Inddnts are handed in to B.W.Os. by Quartermasters or Q.M.Sgts. and checked in their presence, any amendments found necessary being made on the spot. Indents for Bulk Stores must be handed in by the evening previous to the day the wire is despatched. Detail indents come in with the others and are sent to the Base the same day. As far as possible our Units do not mix the two, but if they do, the Bulk items are extracted and the detail indents are then brought in by the B.W.Os. and checked over by the chief clerk, who, after they have been registered, passed them to me for signature.

The evening preceding the day on which Bulk Stores are wired for, the number of articles required, indent numbers and date are entered in the Bulk Book (Specimen attached marked "D") the figures being struck out of the indent and a small "B" inserted in the first column to denote Bulk. The original copy is then brought in for checking with the chief clerk and signature by me. Any seemingly large demands are enquired into and if necessary a memo sent to the O.C., a copy being attached to the indent together with the reply when received. Duplicate copies of indents for Detail Stores are then filed away in separate pads, one for each Unit marked "Incomplete Indents". The total Bulk Issues are abstracted from the B.W.Os. and Sergt. Clerk's (Who looks after distribution of stores) books into the Bulk Wires Book (Specimen attached marked "E") who, in issuing give preference to small demands and then allocate the remainder to the various Units, according to demands. The stores are placed into bays or sacks, whichever is most convenient for existing facilities for drawing or delivering the stores, the items being detailed in A.B.108. Detail stores are treated in like manner except that packages are not opened and no entry is made in A.B.108. The person who receives the stores gives his signature on A.B.108 for Bulk Stores and on the duplicate of the Base I.V. for Detail. One copy of A.B.108 and the original of Base I.V. is given with the stores, the latter for completion and return to the Base Depot.

Stores on payment for Officers are received from the Sgt. Clerk with the vouchers in quadruplicate, the number and date are entered on the duplicate copy of indent and the vouchers then passed to the office for preparation of A.F.W.3225. On presentation of the latter duly completed by the officer concerned, the stores are handed over ~~to the Officer concerned~~ together with one copy of the Base I.V. signed by D.A.D.O.S.

Each day the Bulk Book is completed according to numbers received and issued; the numbers of articles received are placed under the numbers demanded and the quantity or number issued to the Unit is ringed. The No. and date of A.B.108 is then inserted in the columns provided (See"D"). The balance of stores not issued is carried down for inclusion in the next week's demand. The copies of incompleted detail indents are marked up from the duplicate copies of Base I.Vs. The items on the copies of the Bulk incompleted indents are struck out of the indent with blue pencil when issue is made. No receipt number or date is added as the information is all to be found in the Bulk Book. When all items have been marked up the copy of indent is either filed for further action or "P.A." as follows:- "Stores to replace U/S" in a pad to await return of U/S stores, "Stores ~~to replace~~ on payment" in a pad to be checked with A.F.W.~~3225~~ 3069, (a copy of which is sent to me by Units every month); "First Supply", "Expendable" and "Officers on payment", Indents are "P.A." at once.

The unserviceable stores are handed over to the A.O.D. representative at the U/S dump. He prepares A.B.108 in triplicate, bearing a consecutive number and date, for stores accepted by him as unserviceable. The original copy is handed to Unit's representative, the duplicate to the B.W.O. concerned, the triplicate remaining in the book.

An A.B. 129, ruled as per attached "X" is kept by each B,W.O. and the Sergt. Clerk. In this the Principal Bulk Items are posted from the copy of A.B. 108 received from the U/S dump. Detail items appearing on the 108 are marked up on the copy of indent direct. (See indent marked "Y" attached).

At the end of each month, the totals in the U/S book are compared with the monthly issues in the Dues Out Book and any serious difference in numbers issued and received is made out the subject of correspondence with the O.C. responsible. Should the numbers compare favourably, the indent is marked up as shown on "Z" attached and the indent "P.A." The object of keeping a book is to facilitate checking the numbers of garments etc., returned, this method being considered more satisfactory than making several entries on the indent. One is able to ascertain at a glance whether Units are returning the U/S immediately on receipt of new and not accumulating stocks. In my original scheme I did not use a book, but one of my B.W.Os. started it and they all use one now. It does not take them a quarter of an hour a day to look after.

A "Dues Out Book" is kept by each B.W.O. and the Sergt. Clerk, and I prefer it to your pro forma "C". It is completed after each Bulk Demand has been forwarded, the current issue and outstanding demand being entered at the same time. A specimen page marked "F" with explanatory notes is attached.

(Sd) N.DODDS.

Capt.

5-6-17 D.A.D.O.S.,59th. Division.

Special Bulk

INDENT FOR ORDNANCE STORES.

ARMY FORM G. 994.
(In books of 150.)

Indent No. [illegible] Date [illegible] Corps A

To be sent to [illegible] To arrive by

I certify that the following articles are actually required to complete to authorised scale:—
(a) As a first supply; (b) To replace others lost through the exigencies of the service;
(c) To replace others rendered unserviceable through the exigencies of the service.

Signed [illegible] Approved for issue.

Commanding [illegible]

For A.O.D. use only.

ISSUE No.

ARTICLES REQUIRED	Quantity	For A.O.D. use		ARTICLES REQUIRED	Quantity	For A.O.D. use	
[illegible]	X	3		[illegible]			
				[illegible]			
[illegible]				[illegible]			
				[illegible]			
[illegible]	X			[illegible]			
[illegible]	X			[illegible]			
[illegible]	X			[illegible]			

Wt. W11978/M1200 25,000 bks. 2/17 J. T. & S. Ltd.

Index Special Bulk

A	E Earcushions 14	I	M Magazines RSM.LE 15	Q
B	F	J	N	R Respirators Horse 18
C	G	K	O	S. Stereoscopes 10 Sprayers Knapsack 13
D	H	L Lamps Sig. Daylight 17	P. Panniers Signalling 3 Protractors Kit Scale 5	T Insts Telegraph 4

B

CERTIFIED that all indents have been reviewed, those for stores not required, cancelled and outstanding indents hastened.

	Signature of Qmr.	Signature of B.W.O.
April.		
May.		
June.		
July.		
August.		
September.		
October.		
November.		
December.		
January.		
February.		
March.		

C

" RANGEFINDERS INFANTRY "

Indent No.	Unit.	Demand.	I.V.No. & date.	No. issu
20/2339	2/7 Notts & Derby Regt.	1	K/6337 26/4/17	1

BULK BOOK. A.B.124.

Unit.	Indent No.	Date.	Axes Felling.	Axes hand	Bottles Water.	Cordage lbs.		A.B. No.	Date.
2/5 Notts & D. Rgt. 2/8 do.	59/4 59/16	16/3 17/3	(2)	(5)	(4) 6	(3) ~~12~~ 9		D/16 D/20	24/3 25/3
No. Demanded. No. Recd. from Base.		20/3 24/3	2 2	5 5	10 4	12 3			
2/8 Notts & D. Rgt.	59/16	17/3			6	9			

Figure ringed denotes full issue has been made.
" crossed out with (3) beside it, denotes part issue of 3 and 9 carried down.

BULK WIRES BOOK

E

BRIGADE	BULK WIRE & BASE 1V 16	BRASSARDS	SUIT CURTAINS	GLOVES WORSTED	GLOVES FINGER-LESS	DUBBIN 3 oz TINS	LACES 30"	LACES 50"	SOCKS PAIRS	TOWELS HAND	BODY BANDS	BOOTS ANKLE PAIRS 4	5	6	7	8	9	10	11
Divisional Troops			41				2							1	2	9	4	6	6
76 Brigade			2404			1094	642		4										
177 "		9	542			1300								22	21	42	1	8	5
178 "			919			250													
Total		9	3794			2644	642		4					[illegible]	24	49	11	14	11
Stock		-	-			-	-		-					[illegible]	6	50	1	-	-
Demanded	54/24	9	3794			2644	642		4					-	-	-	11	14	11
Received	[illegible]	9	4000			-	642		4					-	-	-	10	14	11
Divisional Troops			41				2					2	3	21	3	7	10	6	6
76 Brigade			2404				640		4										
177 "			542											22	21	42	1	8	5
178 "			919																

" DUES OUT BOOK " A.B. 129

ROPES HEAD HEMP WITH RING.

666

Unit.	B.F.	Demands wk. ending. 6/6	13/6	10/4	Mar.	Apl.	May.	June	etc.	Issues wk. ending 6/4	13/4	20/4	
H.Q.178 Bde.		50	80	80		150				50	30	70	
2/5 Notts.& D.													
2/6 do.	50			50									
2/7 do.													
2/8 do.		50	40			120				50	70		
No.4.Co.A.S.C .													
3rd.Fd.Ambulance.													
470 Co. R.E.			10			10					10		
178 T.M.B.													
174 M.G.C.													
H.Q.D.A.C.													
No.1 Sec. DAC.		100				100				100			
" 2 " "													
B. Ech. "													
Z/Med.T.M.B.													

Figures in left hand columns are numbers demanded. When cross ed through, signifies issue in full is made, the No. issued is entered in corresponding right hand column. The figures in R.H. cols. are totalled & placed under monthly col. as shown, pencilled figures are then erased. The difference between cols. is entered in Bring Forward Col. at beginning of each month.

2/6 Notts and Derby Regt.

A.B. 108 No.	Date.	Jacket S.D.	Tr'sers S.D.	Pant'oons pairs.	Puttees prs.	Boots ankle prs.	Caps S.D.	Gt. Coat.	Grnd. Shts.	Bott-les W'tr
16	12/5	10	10	5	30				10	
26	18/5	25		5		63	10	2		
30	26/5	17	15		10	14				15
33	30/5	14	11	3		10		3	2	
		66	36	13	40	87	10	5	12	15

Y

INDENT FOR ORDNANCE STORES.

ARMY FORM G. 994.
(In books of 150.)

Indent No. [illegible] Date 3/5/17 Corps [illegible]

To be sent to ______ To arrive by ______

For A.O.D. use only.

ISSUE No.

I certify that the following articles are actually required to complete to authorized scale:—
(a) As a first supply; (b) To replace others lost through the exigencies of the service;
(c) To replace others rendered unserviceable through the exigencies of the service.

Signed [illegible] Approved for issue.

Commanding [illegible] Notts & Derby Regt

ARTICLES REQUIRED	Quantity	For A.O.D. use		ARTICLES REQUIRED	Quantity	For A.O.D. use	
[illegible] Draught		6526 10/5/17	7041 13/5				
No. 17	X	1		Ret 11/5		3/8	
Bars Supporting							
Draught Pole [illegible]	X		1	Ret 17/5		4/0	

Wt. W11078/M1200 25,000 bks. 1/17 J. T. & S. Ltd.

Z

INDENT FOR ORDNANCE STORES.

ARMY FORM G. 994.
(In books of 150.)

Indent No. 7/Ind Date 5-8-17 Corps 2/6 Notts & Derby Ref

To be sent to ______ To arrive by ______

For A.O.D. use only.

ISSUE No.

I certify that the following articles are actually required to complete to authorized scale:—
(a) As a first supply; (b) To replace others lost through the exigencies of the service;
(c) To replace others rendered unserviceable through the exigencies of the service.

Signed 2/6 Notts & Derby Ref Approved for issue.

Commanding ______

ARTICLES REQUIRED	Quantity	For A.O.D. use		ARTICLES REQUIRED	Quantity	For A.O.D. use	
Jackets S.D.	4				66 rec		
Trousers S.D.	4				36 rec		
Puttees	4				40 rec		

Wt. W11978/M1208 25,000 bks. 1/17 J. T. & S. Ltd.

Vol 6

CONFIDENTIAL

WAR DIARY OF D.A.D.O.S

59th DIVISION

FROM JULY 1st 1917

TO JULY 31st 1917

VOLUME 6.

Instructions regarding War Diaries and Intelligence Summaries are contained in F. S. Regs., Part II. and the Staff Manual respectively. Title pages will be prepared in manuscript.

WAR DIARY

~~or~~

~~INTELLIGENCE SUMMARY~~.

(Erase heading not required.)

Army Form C. 2118.

Place	Date	Hour	Summary of Events and Information	Remarks and references to Appendices
	1917. July. 1.		Attended conference at Office of A.D.O.S., 111. Corps. Visited all Staff Captains.	
	2 to 7		Routine.	
	8		Attended conference at Office of A.D.O.S., 111. Corps.	
	9		Routine.	
	10		Addressed conference at 176 Brigade H.Qrs. on general questions appertaining to Ordnance.	
	11		Moved Store to O.21.-D.1.8.	
	12		Moved Office to O.21.-D.1.8.	
	13		Routine.	
	14		Called on A.D.O.S. 1V. Corps.	
	15 to 18.		Visited all Staff Captains & inspected all Quartermasters' Stores.	
	19		Conductor Richardson proceeded to England on Ordinary Leave till 29th. ~~June~~. July.	
	20		Routine.	
	21		A.D.O.S. 1V. Corps called.	
	22-3		Routine.	
	24		Divisional Armourers' Shop re-opened. 028372 Pte. G. Turnbull A.O.C. arrived from Ordnance Companies, Havre.	
	25		7142 Pte. R.F. Croft, left to join Ordnance Companies, Havre, pending arrangements for transfer to Infantry.	
	26-8		Routine.	
	29		Conductor Richardson returned off leave.	
	30		Attended demonstration on use of Yukon Back, at H.Qrs. V1. Corps.	
	31		Visited Third Army Laundry, Beauvais.	

S Dodds Capt
D.A.D.O.S.
59th Divn

A5834 Wt. W4973/M687 750,000 8/16 D. D. & L. Ltd. Forms/C.2118/13.

CONFIDENTIAL.

Vol 7

WAR DIARY

OF

DADOS 59TH DIVISION

From 1st August 1917 To 31st August 1917

Volume

CONFIDENTIAL

Instructions regarding War Diaries and Intelligence Summaries are contained in F. S. Regs., Part II. and the Staff Manual respectively. Title pages will be prepared in manuscript.

WAR DIARY
or
~~INTELLIGENCE SUMMARY.~~
(Erase heading not required.)

Army Form C. 2118.

Place	Date	Hour	Summary of Events and Information	Remarks and references to Appendices
August	1.		Routine.	
	2.		G.O.C. 59th Division called and inspected camp, store and workshop. Capt. J.F.D.Dimock, 59th Divisional Laundry and Baths Officer, (attached to D.A.D.O.S. for rations) submitted plan to Division for standard bath. Copy attached marked X.	X
	3.		Routine.	
	4.		Addressed representatives of 176th Brigade including Coy. Com. and C.Q.M.S. and gave demonstration on use of Yukon Pack. No.031879 Private J.L.Higman arrived for duty from Ord.Coy.Havre.	
	5.		Addressed representatives of 178th Brigade including Coy.Com. and C.Q.M.S. and gave demonstration on use of Yukon Pack.	
	6.		Addressed representatives of 177th Brigade including Coy. Com. and C.Q.M.S. and gave demonstration on use of Yukon Pack No.026100 Private A.Rodhouse admitted to Hospital.	
	7.		Visited all Staff Captains. A.D.O.S. 1V.Corps called. No.7146 S/Cdr.J.R.Akass left for ordinary leave to England.	
	8.		Routine. No.026100 Pte.A.Rodhouse evacuated to Base.	
	9.		A.D.O.S., 1V.Corps called.	
	10-12.		Routine.	
	13-17.		Visited all Staff Captains.	
	18-19.		Routine.	

A5834 Wt. W4973/M687 750,000 8/16 D. D. & L. Ltd. Forms/C.2118/13.

Instructions regarding War Diaries and Intelligence Summaries are contained in F. S. Regs., Part II. and the Staff Manual respectively. Title pages will be prepared in manuscript.

WAR DIARY
or
INTELLIGENCE SUMMARY.
(Erase heading not required.)

Army Form C. 2118.

Place	Date	Hour	Summary of Events and Information	Remarks and references to Appendices
August	20.		Routine. No.7146 S/Ddr.R.J.Akass returned from ordinary leave to England.	
	21.		D.D.O.S. III Army called and inspected stores; also interviewed B.W.O's and Sergt. Reynolds. A.D.O.S. IV. Corps called.	
	22-24.		Routine.	
	25.		A.D.O.S. IV, Corps called.	
	26.		Routine.	
	27.		No.206819 Pte.J.R.Leaver and No.274243 Pte.W.Dickinson returned to their Units - 59th Divisional Supply Column. No.189434 Pte.H.Finn and No.273846 Pte.F.T.Bates reported for duty from 59th Divisional Supply Column.	
	28.		A.D.O.S. IV.Corps called. Application for brushes for use with machine invented by Capt.J.F.D.Dimock,2/8 Notts & Derby Regt., 59th Divisional Laundry and Baths Officer, for brushing eggs from shirts forwarded to A.D.O.S. (Copy attached). No02673 S/Cdr.D.Jones proceeded to England on ordinary leave. D.A.D.O.S. proceeded with Laundry Officer to Winnezeele.	Y
	29.		Closed Office and store at Rocquigny. Staff proceeded with lorries to Albert.	
	30.		Moved staff and lorries from Albert to Winnezeele J17.A.5.4.(Sht. No.27) Visited Acting A.D.O.S. XIX.Corps.	
	31.		Opened Office and Store at Winnezeele. J17.A5.4. (Sht.No.27).	

J Dodd Lieut
D.A.D.O.S. 59th Divn

A5834 Wt. W4973/M687 750,000 8/16 D. D. & L. Ltd. Forms/C.2118/13.

Suggested Plan for Standard Plunge & Shower Bath

Scale 8 feet to 1 inch.

X

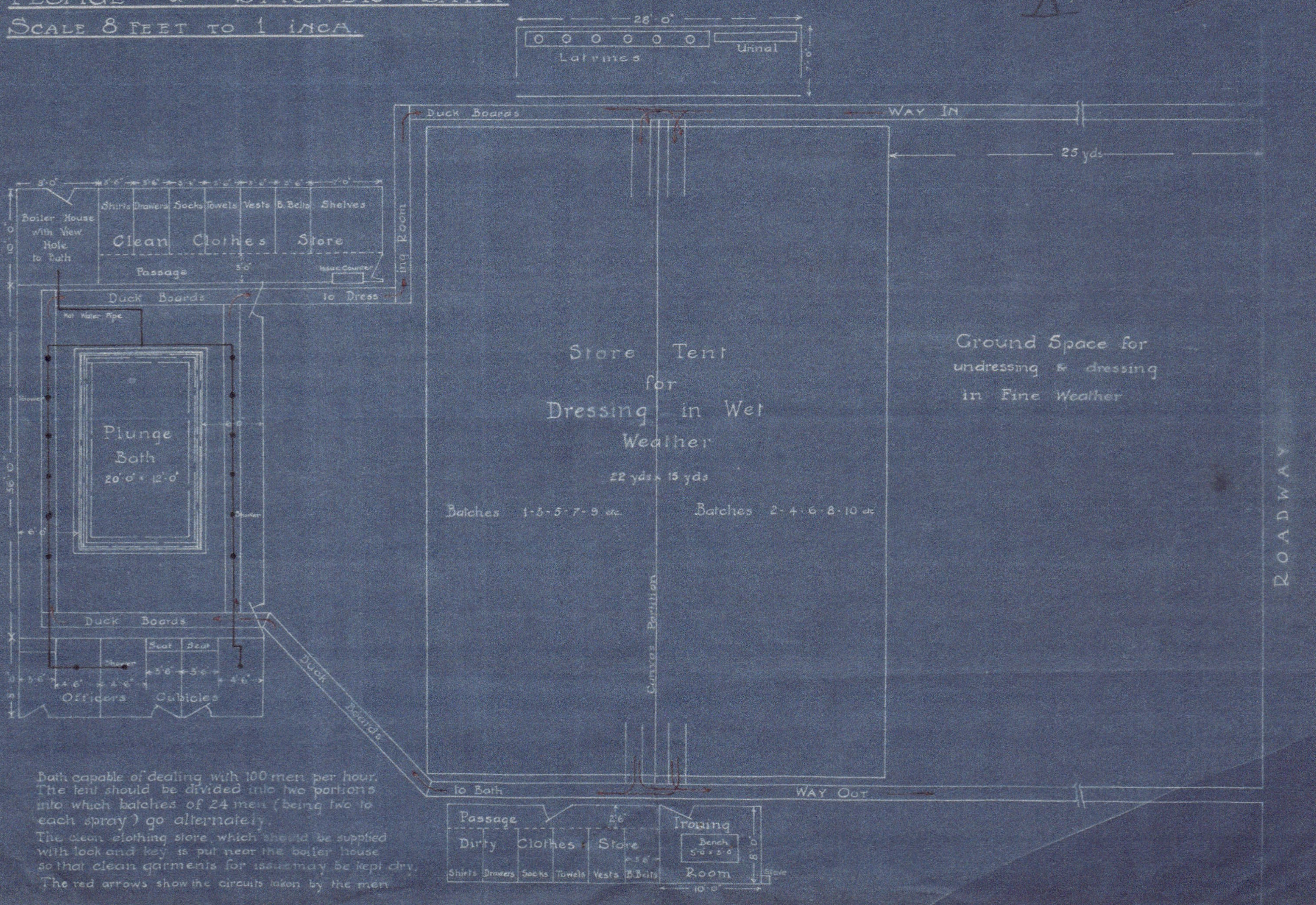

Bath capable of dealing with 100 men per hour. The tent should be divided into two portions into which batches of 24 men (being two to each spray) go alternately.

The clean clothing store which should be supplied with lock and key is put near the boiler house so that clean garments for issue may be kept dry.

The red arrows show the circuits taken by the men.

COPY.

Y

D.A.D.O.S.,

59th Division.

As you are aware, a machine has been on test in the Divisional Laundry for a month past for the brushing of shirts to free them from eggs. The machine now in existence (made out of an unserviceable bicycle) is worked by a pedal arrangement geared so that the velocity on a circular wire brush is maintained at 650 revolutions per minute. It has been found that with two brushes on the machine - a man working at each - it is possible to clean three times as many shirts as can be done in the same time by three man with hand brushes. The machine has been so made that it is possible to work 4 or 6 or even more brushes with one man to pedal for them all. With six brushes and a man to pedal it would be possible to clean 750 shirts in a day instead of 150 with the hand brushes.

Under these circumstances I am writing to ask if it is possible for these circular wire brushes to be obtained through you or in the alternative, for permission to be obtained for them to be purchased in England. The brushes now in use were purchased by me from the N Dental Manufacturing Company and are a standard make used by Dental Mechanics on treddle machines. They are called 'Wire Burr Brushes' and are 2" diameter over all. The length of the wire bristles is ½" and the brushes are very closely packed. The inner diameter for the spindle is 3/16ths inch. The wire is of steel but thinner than the wire put in the hand brushes and the cost from the Company is now 3/6 each.

In addition to the above facts, I should like to point out that with the brush running at 650 revolutions per minute, it is not necessary to apply the shirt with any pressure on the brush (which pressure is always necessary with the hand brush) and the damage to the shirtis not so great as is brought about with a handbrush being worked right into the seams of the garment.

The D.A.D.M.S, of the III Army saw the machine working on Friday last, and expressed his approval and took notes.

I should be glad if you will let me have 12 brushes made or supplied as soon as possible. If necessary, I can let you have a brush as a sample. May I state further that circular brushes made of ordinary bristles of different strengths have been tried on the machine but they are not found to be satisfactory.

You will remember that by the introduction of my idea of placing steam distributing pipes into the cages of the drums of the Thresh Disinfactor we were able to quicken the turnover in the Laundry considerably and so save the necessity of increasing the stock. The M.T. Inspector of steam vehicles saw the pipes at work the otherday and informed me that he is going to have them introduced into all Foden Disinfectors in the country. I hope with the above brushing arrangement to further speed up the turnover so that the Laundry may run with as small a stock as possible and with improved results. For a considerable time now all shirts with eggs coming from the Laundry have been brushed before issue, ~~and~~ before the brushing machine was made it was very difficult to cope with this very necessary part of the Laundry work.

(sd) J.F.D.Dimock.
Capt.
28-8-17. Laundry Officer, 59th Division.

A.D.O.S., IV. Corps.

Can the brushes required be obtained through Ordnance please. Capt. Dimock's device is a great saver of labour and I think of shirts.

(sd) J.Dodds.
Capt.
28-8-17. D.A.D.O.S., 59th Division.

CONFIDENTIAL.

Vol 8

WAR DIARY

OF

D.A.D.O.S. 59TH DIVISION.

FROM SEPT. 1ST 1917 TO SEPT 30TH 1917.

Instructions regarding War Diaries and Intelligence Summaries are contained in F. S. Regs., Part II. and the Staff Manual respectively. Title Pages will be prepared in manuscript.

WAR DIARY
or
INTELLIGENCE SUMMARY
(Erase heading not required.)

Army Form C. 2118

Place	Date	Hour	Summary of Events and Information	Remarks and references to Appendices
	Sept.			
	1.		Routine.	
	2.		No.011382, Pte. W.E.Hicken reported for duty from Ordnance Havre.	
	3.		Lt. W.Foster, M.C. 2/7 Notts & Derby Regt. reported for instructional duty. Auth.G.R.O., O.B.132 17-8-17.	
	4.		Visited all Staff Captains.	
	5.		Lt. W.Foster, M.C. 2/7 Notts & Derby Regt. returned from instructional duty to 178th Brigade.	
	6.		Visited Staff Captain 176th Brigade.	
	7.		Visited all Staff Captains; also A.D.O.S. XIX Corps.	
	8.		Major, The Hon. J.N.Ridley, Northumberland Hussars reported for instructional duty. Auth. G.R.O., O.B.132. d/- 17-8-17.	
			No.02673, S/Cdr. Jones, D. returned from Ordinary leave to England.	
			A.D.O.S., V Corps called and inspected stores.	
	9.		Major, The Hon.J.N.Ridley, Northumberland Hussars returned from instructional duty to Head Quarters, 59th Division.	
			No.028372, Pte. Turnbull, G. proceeded on leave to England.	
	10.		Visited Staff Captain 176th Inf. Bde; also A.D.O.S. V Corps.	
			Plan of Capt. J.F.D.Dimock's, 2/8 Notts & Derby Regt. Divl. Laundry & Baths Officer, device for Brushing underclothing sent to A.D.O.S V. Corps. Copy attached. X	X
	11.		Routine.	
	12.		Visited Ordnance Depot, Calais.	
			Capt. J.F.D.Dimock, 2/8 Notts & Derby Regt. Divl. Laundry and Baths Officer, proceeded on leave to England.	
			No.2261 Arm/S/Sgt.Leech and No.2941 Arm/S/Sgt Pegrum temp. attached to V Corps Salvage forduty.	
	13.		Routine.	
	14.		Visited all Staff Captains.	
	15&16.		Routine.	
	17.		Judged Yukon Pack Competition 178th Inf. Bde.	
	18.		Judged Yukon Pack Competition 176th Inf. Bde.	
	19.		Arm/S/Sgt. Harris, J. No.2182, proceeded on ordinary leave to Eng:	
			Visited A.D.O.S. V Corps.	
			No.028372, Pte. Turnbull, G. returned from ordinary leave to England	

1875 Wt. W593/826 1,000,000 4/15 J.B.C. & A. A.D.S.S./Forms/C. 2118.

Instructions regarding War Diaries and Intelligence Summaries are contained in F. S. Regs., Part II. and the Staff Manual respectively. Title Pages will be prepared in manuscript.

WAR DIARY
or
INTELLIGENCE SUMMARY
(Erase heading not required.)

Army Form C. 2118

Place	Date	Hour	Summary of Events and Information	Remarks and references to Appendices
	Sept. 20/21.		Routine.	
	22.		Stores transferred from Winnezeele to 18, Place Berthon, Poperinghe.	
	23.		Office transferred from Winnezeele to 18, Place Berthon, Poperinghe.	
	24.		Capt. J.F.D.Dimock, 2/8 Notts & Derby Regt. & Divl. Laundry & Baths Officer returned from ordinary leave to England. A.D.O.S. V Corps called.	
	25/28.		Routine.	
	29.		Visited A.D.O.S. 2nd Anzac Corps.	
	30.		Capt. J. Dodds, D.A.D.O.S. 59th Division, proceeded to No.14 Ordnance Depot for a Course on Ammunition from 1/10/17 to 12/10/17 in accordance with D.D.O.S. V Army letter F.S./179.	

J Dodds
Capt
D.A.D.O.S.
59th Divn

1875 Wt. W593/826 1,000,000 4/15 J.B.C. & A. A.D.S.S./Forms/C. 2118.

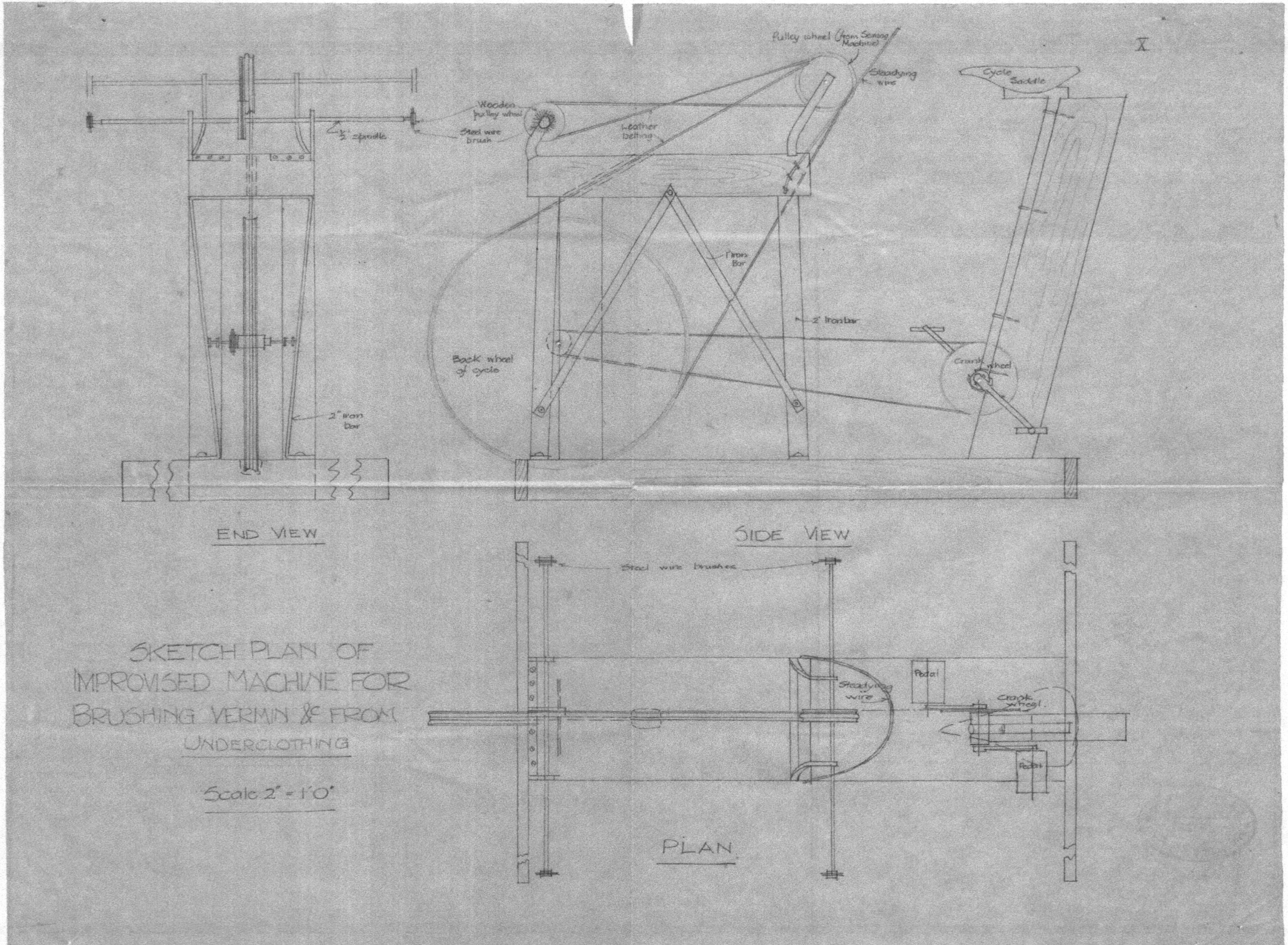
X
Pulley wheel (from Sewing Machine)
Steadying wire
Cycle Saddle
Wooden pulley wheel
Steel wire brush
½" spindle
Leather belting
Iron bar
2" Iron bar
Back wheel of cycle
Crank wheel
2" Iron bar
END VIEW
SIDE VIEW
Steel wire brushes
Pedal
Steadying wire
Crank wheel
Pedal
PLAN
SKETCH PLAN OF
IMPROVISED MACHINE FOR
BRUSHING VERMIN &c FROM
UNDERCLOTHING
Scale 2" = 1'0"

Confidential.

COPY.

X

X.

Capt. J. Dodds, A.O.D. has attended a 10 days' course of instruction here in the Ammunition in use by the British Armies in France, with the following results :-

Work in class	(New to Ammunition. Has displayed intelligence (energy and enthusiasm throughout, and obtained (a capital examination result.
Examination.	Satisfactory.

(Sd) J.F.King.

No.14 Ordnance Depot.
12/10/1917.

Major, A.O.D.
Ordnance Officer.

Instructions regarding War Diaries and Intelligence Summaries are contained in F. S. Regs., Part II. and the Staff Manual respectively. Title pages will be prepared in manuscript.

WAR DIARY
or
INTELLIGENCE SUMMARY.
(Erase heading not required.)

Army Form C. 2118.

Place	Date	Hour	Summary of Events and Information	Remarks and references to Appendices
	1917. Octbr.			
	1.		Store and Office transferred from POPERINGHE Map ref. Hazebrouck 5A I.2.7.3. to STEENBECQUE Map. ref. Hazebrouck 5A, F.4.7.1.	
	2.		Routine.	
	3.		Routine. No.011382, Pte. W.E.Hicken, proceeded on ordinary leave to England.	
	4.		Routine. No.2182, Armr/S/Sgt. J. Harris, returned from ordinary leave to England.	
	5.		Transferred store from STEENBECQUE Map ref. Hazebrouck 5A, F.4.7.1 to GREUPPE map ref. Hazebrouck 5A. C.6.7.7.	
	6.		Transferred Office from STEENBECQUE map ref. Hazebrouck 5A.F.4.7.1 to GREUPPE map ref. Hazebrouck 5A. C.6.7.7.	
	7/10.		Routine.	
	11.		Routine. No.M/281389, Pte. A.E.Eastman, A.S.C.M.T. (attached) returned from ordinary leave to England.	
	12.		Capt. J. Dodds, returned from instructional course, at No.14 Ordnance Depot and took over from A/Condr. S.E.Richardson, No. 5098 who had been acting for him. Copy of report on course attached.	X
	13.		Store transferred from GREUPPE Map ref. Hazebrouck 5A, C.6.7.7. to ESTREE-CAUCHIE Map ref. Sheet 36B. W.2.Central.	
	14.		Office transferred from GREUPPE Map ref. Hazebrouck 5A, C.6.7.7. to ESTREE-CAUCHIE Map.ref. Sheet 36B. W.2.Central.	
	15.		Visited all Staff Captains.	
	16/18.		Routine. (16)No.C11382,Pte.W.E.Hicken returned from leave to England.	
	19.		D.D.O.S. 1st Army and A.D.O.S. V Corps called.	
	20.		Visited all Staff Captains.	
	21.		Commenced transfer of store from ESTREE-CAUCHIE Map ref.Sheet 36B W.2.Central to East of CARENCY Map ref. Sheet 36B.X.17.C.5.9.	
	22.		Continued transfer of store from ESTREE-CAUCHIE Map ref.Sheet 36B W.2.Central to East of CARENCY Map ref. Sheet 36B.X.17.C.5.9.	
	23.		Completed transfer of store from ESTREE-CAUCHIE Map ref.Sheet 36B.W.2.Cent. to East of CARENCY Map ref.Sheet 36B.X.17.C.5.9.	

Army Form C. 2118

Instructions regarding War Diaries and Intelligence Summaries are contained in F. S. Regs., Part II. and the Staff Manual respectively. Title Pages will be prepared in manuscript.

WAR DIARY
or
INTELLIGENCE SUMMARY
(Erase heading not required.)

Place	Date	Hour	Summary of Events and Information	Remarks and references to Appendices
	1917. Octbr. 24.		Transferred office from ESTREE-CAUCHIE Map ref. Sheet 36B. W.2.Central to East of CARENCY Map ref. Sheet 36B X.17.C.5.9.	
	25.		Capt. J. Dodds, proceeded on ordinary leave to England A/Cdr. S.E.Richardson, No.5098 took over as he did on the 19th June 1917. Commenced using Decauville system of transport.	
	26/30		Routine.	

J Dodds Capt
D.A.D.O.S.
59th Div

1875 Wt. W593/826 1,000,000 4/15 J.B.C. & A. A.D.S.S./Forms/C. 2118.

CONFIDENTIAL

Vol 10

War Diary
of
D.A.D.O.S 59th Div.

From 1st November 1917 To 30th November 1917

Volume No. 10

Army Form C. 2118

Instructions regarding War Diaries and Intelligence Summaries are contained in F. S. Regs., Part II. and the Staff Manual respectively. Title Pages will be prepared in manuscript.

WAR DIARY
or
INTELLIGENCE SUMMARY
(Erase heading not required.)

Place	Date	Hour	Summary of Events and Information	Remarks and references to Appendices
1917.				
Novr.	1-4.		Routine.	
	5.		A.D.O.S., Vth Corps called.	
			Capt. J. Dodds returned from Ordinary leave to England.	
	6-8.		Routine.	
	9.		Visited Staff Captain R.A. and 176th Infantry Brigade.	
	10.		Visited Staff Captains 177th and 178th Infantry Brigades.	
	11-15.		Routine.	
	16.		Transferred stores from E. of CARENCY Map reference X.17.C.5.9 Map. 36B to BARLIN Map reference K.33.central Sheet 36B.	
	17.		Transferred office from E. of CARENCY Map reference X.17.C.5.9 Sht.36B to BARLIN Map reference K.33.central Sht.36B.	
	1 8.		Routine.	
	19.		Transferred office and stores from BARLIN Map reference K.33. central Sht.36B to BEAUMETZ LES LOGES Map. refer-ence Sht.Lens 11 Near ARRAS.	
	20-21.		Routine.	
	22.		Transferred office and stores from BEAUMETZ LES LOGES Map reference Sht.Lens near ARRAS to ACHIET LE PETIT Map ref. G.13.B.7.3. Sheet 57C.	
	23.		Transferred office and stores from ACHIET LE PETIT Map. ref. G.13.B.7.3. Sht.57C to NURLU Map ref. V.29.C.0.4. Sht. 57C.	
	24.		Transferred office and stores from NURLU Map ref. V.29.C.0.4. Sht. 57C to ETRICOURT Map ref. V.7.D.9.4. Sht. 57C.	
	25.		Routine.	
	26.		Visited A.D.O.S., III Cor ps.	
			Visited Staff Captains 177th and 178th Infantry Brigades.	
	27.		Visited Staff Captain 176th Infantry Brigade.	
	28.		Routine.	
	29.		D.D.O.S. III Armys called and inspected Office and Stores.	
	30.		Visited A.D.O.S., Vth Corps.	

J Dodds Capt
D.A.D.O.S.
59th Div

1875 Wt. W593/826 1,000,000 4/15 J.B.C. & A. A.D.S.S./Forms/C. 2118.

Confidential.   Vol 11

War Diary
of
D. A. D. O. S. 59th Divn.

From 1st Dec. 1917   To 31st Dec. 1917

Volume No. 10.

Instructions regarding War Diaries and Intelligence Summaries are contained in F. S. Regs., Part II. and the Staff Manual respectively. Title Pages will be prepared in manuscript.

WAR DIARY
or
INTELLIGENCE SUMMARY
(Erase heading not required.)

Army Form C. 2118

Place	Date	Hour	Summary of Events and Information	Remarks and references to Appendices
1917. December	1.		Transferred office and store from ETRICOURT Map ref.V.7.d.9.5. Sht.57C to FREMICOURT Map ref. I.19.d.5.7. Sht.57C.	
	2/5.		Routine.	
	6.		Transferred office and stores from FREMICOURT Map ref.I.19.d.57 Sht.57C to YTRES Map ref.P.26.d.8.3. Sht. 57C.	
	7/8.		Routine.	
	9.		No.S/7146, A/Sub/Cdr.Akass, R.J. transferred for duty with D.A.D.O.S. 29th Divn. No.04127 A/Sub/Cdr. Rochester,H.J.W. reported for duty from 29th Divn.	
	10.		Routine.	
	11.		A.D.O.S.Vth Corps called and inspected office and stores.	
	12.		Visited Staff Captain 176th Infantry Brigade.	
	13.		Lieut.G.B.Oliver, 2/4 Leicester Regt. attached as 'Learner' under Auth. G.H.Q.letter O.B/1329 dated 17/8/17.	
	14/16		Routine.	
	17.		Transferred office and stores from YTRES Map ref.P.26.d.8.3. Sht.57C to BUS Map ref.O.23.d.6.5. Sht.57C.	
	22		Lt.G.B.Oliver, 2/4 Leicester Regt. completed instructional course.	
	18/21		Routine.	
	22.		Transferred stores from BUS Map ref.O.23.d.6.5. Sht. 57C to HOUVIN-HOUVIGNEUL Map ref. H.14.b.5.2. Sht.51C.	
	23.		Transferred office from BUS Map ref.O.23.d.6.5. Sht. 57C to HOUVIN-HOUVIGNEUL Map ref. H.14.b.5.2. Sht.51C.	
	24/26		Routine.	
	27.		Visited Staff Captains 176th and 178th Infy. Bdes.	
	28.		Visited Staff Captain 177th Infy. Bde.	
	29.		Routine.	
	30.		Transferred stores from HOUVIN-HOUVIGNEUL Map ref.H.14.b.5.2 Sht.51C to WAMIN Map ref.H.33.d.4.5. Sht.51C.	
	31.		Transferred office from HOUVIN-HOUVIGNEUL Map ref.H.14.b.5.2 Sht.51C to WAMIN Map ref.H.33.d.4.5. Sht.51C. Opened Artillery Dump at F109,Rue St.Larde, DOULLENS.	

J Woodcraft
D.A.D.O.S. 59 Div.

1875 Wt. W593/826 1,000,000 4/15 J.B.C. & A. A.D.S.S./Forms/C. 2118.

Instructions regarding War Diaries and Intelligence Summaries are contained in F. S. Regs., Part II. and the Staff Manual respectively. Title Pages will be prepared in manuscript.

WAR DIARY
or
INTELLIGENCE SUMMARY
(Erase heading not required.)

DADOS. 59 D

Army Form C. 2118

Vol 12

Place	Date	Hour	Summary of Events and Information	Remarks and references to Appendices
1918. Jany.	1-4.		Routine.	
	5.		Visited Staff Captain 177th Infy. Bde.	
	6-8.		Visited all Staff Captains and Artillery Units.	
	8-14.		Routine.	
	15.		Visited Staff Captain R.A.	
	16.		Visited all Units.	
	17.		A.D.O.S. VIth Corps called and inspected Office and stores. A/2184, Armr/Sgt/Major A.E.Stanbridge proceeded on Ordy. leave to England.	
	18.		No.04971, Sergt.E.Douglas reported for duty from No.8 Ord. Depot.	
	19.		No.09922, Pte. G.H.Dutfield, proceeded on Ordy. leave to England.	
	20-23.		Routine.	
	24.		Visited all Staff Captains.	
	25-26.		Routine.	
	27.		Visited all Staff Captains.	
	28.		No.08844,L/Cpl. W.Sharratt and No.012597,Pte. L.Quinn proceeded on Ordy. leave to England.	
	29.		Routine. No.02673, Sub/Cdr. D.Jones reported for duty from No.10 Canadian Hospital, ST.POL.	
	30.		Attended Conference at A.D.O.S. VIth Corps. Capt. R.S.Tennent reported for duty as 'Learner! Auth.G.H.Q. letter No.OB/1329 dated 17th Aug. 1917.	
	31.		Capt.R.S.Tennent completed duty as 'Learner' and returned to Divl. H.Qrs.	

J Dodds
Capt
DADOS
59th Div

1875 Wt. W593/826 1,000,000 4/15 J.B.C. & A. A.D.S.S./Forms/C. 2118.

Confidential

Vol 13

War Diary
of
D. A. D. O. S. 59th Divn.

From 1st Feb. 1918 — To 28th Feb. 1918

Volume No. 13.

Instructions regarding War Diaries and Intelligence Summaries are contained in F. S. Regs., Part II. and the Staff Manual respectively. Title Pages will be prepared in manuscript.

WAR DIARY
or
INTELLIGENCE SUMMARY
(Erase heading not required.)

Army Form C. 2118

Place	Date	Hour	Summary of Events and Information	Remarks and references to Appendices
1918. February.	1.		No.02673, Sgt.D.Jones proceeded to HAVRE for duty.	
	2.		Routine.	
	3.		No.S/5847,T/S/Cdr.WJ.Downing reported for duty from Ordce. Vth Cav. Divn.	
	4.		No.A/2184, Armr/S/Major Stanbridge A.E. and No.09922 Pte. Dutfield G.H.returned from Ordinary leave to England.	
	5-10.		Routine.	
	11.		Transferred stores from WAMIN Map ref.H.33.d.4.5.Sht.51C to ERVILLERS Map ref.B.13.d.3.7. Sht.57C. No.09922,Pte.G.H.Dutfield proceeded to VI Cps.for temp. duty.	
	12.		Transferred Office from WAMIN Map ref.H.33.d.4.5.Sht.51C to ERVILLERS Map ref.B.13.d.3.7. Sht.57C.	
	13.		No.S/5098,Cdr.S.E.Richardson proceeded on Ordy.leave to England.	
			No.08844,L/Cpl.W.Sharratt returned from Ordy. leave to England.	
	14.		No.012597,Pte.Quinn,L.V. do do do	
	15.		Routine.	
	16.		No.018597,Pte.Willie,F.C.proceeded on Ordy. leave to England.	
	17.		Routine.	
	18.		Capt.A.W.Viret, A.O.D.Reported for temporary attachment from Ordce. HAVRE.	
			No.09922,Pte.Dutfield GH. returned from Ordce.VIth Corps.	
	19.		No.04971,Sergt.Douglas, E. appointed to rank of A/S/Cdr.with pay and allowances from 16/1/18.Auth.W.C.Orders 481 d/- 19/1/18.	
	20.		Visited all Staff Captains.	
	21.		Routine.	
	22.		No.08844,L/Cpl.Sharratt W, proceeded to G.HQ.for duty with D.O.S. Auth.D.D.O.S.III Army wire ZF/167 D/- 21/2/18.	
	23-25.		Routine.	
	26.		Capt.A.W.Viret, AOD completed tempy.attachment and returned to Ordnance HAVRE.	
	27.		Routine.	
	28.		Visited A.D.O.S., VIth Corps.	

S Dodds Capt
DADOS
59 Div

1875 Wt. W593/826 1,000,000 4/15 J.B.C. & A. A.D.S.S./Forms/C. 2118.

Instructions regarding War Diaries and Intelligence Summaries are contained in F. S. Regs., Part II. and the Staff Manual respectively. Title Pages will be prepared in manuscript.

WAR DIARY
or
INTELLIGENCE SUMMARY
(Erase heading not required.)

Army Form C. 2118

Place	Date	Hour	Summary of Events and Information	Remarks and references to Appendices
1918			Sheet No. 2.	
March	28.	a.m.	Transferred Office and stores from FIENVILLERS to LABEUVRIERE.	
		p.m.	Transferred Office and stores from LABEUVRIERE to MONGOVAL.	
	29.		Visited ADOS, 1st Corps (to whom attached instead of 13th Corps) arranged to send a Bulk indent for general stores to CALAIS which I did. Also wired to Gun Park for Vickers and Lewis Guns.	
	30.		ADOS, 13th Corps called the Division having been transferred to 13th Corps for administration.	
			Copies of correspondence with ADOS, VIth Corps re stores returned to Base and difficulties of open warfare from Ordnance point of view attached marked:-	X and Y.
	31.		Routine.	
			During past few days about 40 Vickers and 53 Lewis Guns issued to Units. 41 additional Lewis guns drawn from Gun Park but 177th Infy. Brigade refused to accept delivery.	
			J Dodds Capt D.A.D.O.S. 59th Div	

Instructions regarding War Diaries and Intelligence Summaries are contained in F. S. Regs., Part II. and the Staff Manual respectively. Title Pages will be prepared in manuscript.

WAR DIARY
or
INTELLIGENCE SUMMARY
(Erase heading not required.)

DA.D.O.S. 59 Divn

Vol 14

Army Form C. 2118

Place	Date	Hour	Summary of Events and Information	Remarks and references to Appendices
1918				
March	1.		No.S/5098,Condr.S.E.Richardson returned from leave to England.	
			No.025473,Pte.W.J.McCarthy, proceeded on leave to England.	
			No.04971,S/Cdr.E.Douglas, evacuated to No.6 Stationary Hospital.	
	2.		Routine.	
	3.		Capt.J.Dodds proceeded on leave to England.	
			No.271125,Tpr.J.P.Nolan proceeded on leave to England.	
	4.		No.028591,Pte.F.C.Willie, returned from leave to England.	
	5.		Routine.	
	6.		A.D.O.S.,VI Corps inspected Office and stores.	
	7.		No.030401,Pte.A.W.Farthing,reported for duty from Ordce.HAVRE. Auth.A.O.C.Rein.1059/182 dated 1/3/18.	
	8-15.		Routine.	
	16.		No.A/2258,Armr/S/Sgt.FS.Hutchinson proceeded on leave to England.	
			A.D.O.S.,VI Corps called and inspected Office and stores.	
	17.		Routine.	
	18.		No.025473,Pte.W.J.McCarthy returned from leave to England.	
			Capt.Dodds returned from leave to England.	
			No.271125,Tpr.J.P.Nolan returned from leave to England.	
	19.		No.03208,S/Cdr.W.G.Valentine reported for duty from 3rd Cav.Divn.	
	20.		Routine.	
	21.		Transferred Office and stores from ERVILLERS to BUCQUOY.	
	22.		Routine.	
	23.		Transferred Office and stores from BUCQUOY to BOUZINCOURT.	
	24.		Routine.	
	25.		Transferred Office and stores from BOUZINCOURT to CONTAY.	
	26.		Transferred Office and stores from CONTAY TO FIENVILLERS.	
	27.		Visited DDOS (South) at ABBEVILLE re the refitting of the Division. Wired ADOS,1st Corps our probable requirements of Vickers and Lewis guns.	
	28.		Saw ADOS,1st Corps who informed me the Division was being attached to 13th Corps. He promised to wire the ADOS,13th Corps re our Vickers and Lewis Guns; also Gas reserves.	

A.D.O.S., VIth Corps. Sheet No.2.

(1). For Detail of stores see above.

(2). NIL.

(3). NIL. I do not consider that the gas stores come under this category.

J Dodds

Capt.
D.A.D.O.S., 59th Division.

30-3-18.

SECRET.

G.C.201/1.

D.A.D.O.S.,
59th Division.

Will you please let me have a short description of kind and tonnage of stores :-

(1). Returned to Base.
(2). Abandoned or destroyed.
(3). Abandoned on first move, but subsequently recovered.

since 21st instant.

(sd). J.E.Courtice.

Lt.Colonel.

27-3-18. A.D.O.S., VIth Corps.
EC.

-2-

A.D.O.S.,
VIth Corps.

With reference to your G.C.201/1 of 27-3-18.

On receiving the order to remove from ERVILLERS to BUCQUOY I took the whole of the stores back in three journeys, the majority of the staff working all night.

On arrival at BUCQUOY, forseeing that there was a probability of another move, I sent the undermentioned stores to the base:-

S.B.Respirators.	411.	Containers (N.C)	2140.
Vermorel Sprayers.	2.	Vacuum Bulbs.	12.
Trench fans.	224.	Strombus horns.	3.
Air cylinders.	42.	S.horn pipes.	10.
Rattles.	52.	Horse Respirators.	14.

Jackets S.D.	25.	Pantaloons prs.	17.
Buckets water canvas.	77.	Blankets G.S.	16.
Hooks bill.	7.	Imps. int.tool heads.	4.
Bags ration.	112.	Tins Mess. D.S.	4.
Bags nose G.S.	148.	Brushes dandy.	6.
" " large.	49.	Chains collar.	21.
Boxes horse shoes.	14.		
" frost cogs.	8.		
Bicycles.	12. These were received from Units and undergoing repair.		
Stoves Soyers.	14.		
Suits overalls for raiding parties.	100.		
Poles draught No.7.	1. and 6 sacks, 17 bundles or bags of sundry detail stores of minor value.		

On arrival at BOUZINCOURT I had to send one lorry and the necessary staff to 40th Division to which my Artillery were transferred. I therefore, left the gas reserves at the latter place.

On arrival at CONTAY I send back immediately for the gas reserves; and as I was unable to carry them, sent them to the Base via VILLERS BRETONEAUX Railhead.

Date of Arrival in VI Corps Area.	Place.	Date of Departure.	Move to.
In Area at opening of attack.	ERVILLERS.	21/3/18.	BUCQUOY.
	BUCQUOY	23/3/18.	BOUZINCOURT.
	BOUZINCOURT.	25/3/18.	CONTAY.
	CONTAY.	26/3/18.	FEINVILLERS.

X

D.A.D.O.S., 3rd Division.
D.A.D.O.S., 31st Division.
D.A.D.O.S., 34th Division.
D.A.D.O.S., 40th Division.
D.A.D.O.S., 42nd Division. -1-
D.A.D.O.S., 59th Division.
D.A.D.O.S., Guards Division.

Please keep a record of all movements of your unit whilst with this formation and forward particulars to me in the event of your leaving this Corps.

Details wanted are:-

Date of arrival in VI Corps Area.	Place.	Date of departure.	Move to.

I do not want a long description, but require details to enable me to know exactly the defficulties of open warfare.

(sd). J.E.Courtice.
Lt.Colonel.
27/3/18. A.D.O.S., VIth Corps.
EC.

-2-

A.D.O.S.,
VIth Corps.

Date/&c. of moves are attached as per your pro forma:-
For fuller information see reply to your G.C.201/1.

With Armourer's Shops and the necessary equipment, gas stores, personnel to run the 'U' dump, cooks, servant, tents, cooking utensils &c. the D.A.D.O.S. is more or less immobile, especially if he has to detach a lorry to go with the Artillery, to another Divisio If advancing, he can drop the Armourers and 'U' dump personnel; if retiring, he must get rid of almost all stores - at least that is my opinion.

It was only by the willing co-operation and hard work of all my staff that I was able to save every item I had on my dump and in my office.

J Dodds
Capt.
30/3/18. D.A.D.O.S., 59th Division.

Confidential

Vol 15

War Diary
of
D. A. D. O. S. 59th Divn.

From 1st April 1918 — To 30th April 18

Volume No. 18.

Army Form C. 2118.

Instructions regarding War Diaries and Intelligence Summaries are contained in F. S. Regs., Part II. and the Staff Manual respectively. Title pages will be prepared in manuscript.

WAR DIARY
or
INTELLIGENCE SUMMARY.
(Erase heading not required.)

Place	Date	Hour	Summary of Events and Information	Remarks and references to Appendices
1918. APRIL.	1.		Routine.	
	2.		Transferred Office and Stores from MINGOVAL to PROVEN.	
	2.		Proceeded to CALAIS re refitting of units, 8 lorries following me in the early morning.	
	3.		Eight lorry loads of stores received from CALAIS. Staff worked all night 3/4th receiving and preparing stores for units.	
	4.		Visited Staff Captains.	
	5.		Transferred Office and stores from PROVEN to BRANDHOEK.	
	6/7.		Routine.	
	8.		A.D.O.S., VIII Corps called and inspected Office and stores.	
	9.		Visited Staff Captains.	
	10.		Divisional Commander called to thank the staff for good work done during recent operations, specially mentioning the promptitude with which the division had been re-equipped.	
	11.		Commenced return of Winter clothing.	
	12.		A.D.O.S., VIII Corps called.	
	13.		Transferred Office and Stores from BRANDHOEK to WATOU.	
	14/18.		Routine.	
	19.		Transferred Office and Stores from WATOU to "J" Camp, Map ref. A.8.C.3.6. Sheet 28.	
	20.		Routine.	
	21.		Transferred Office and Stores from "J" Camp Map ref. A.8.C.3.6. Sht.28 to BAMBECQUE Map ref. V.29.C.8.4. Sht.19.	
	22.		Visited all Staff Captains. Visited A.D.O.S., VIII Corps.	
	23.		Visited all Staff Captains.	
	24/25.		Routine.	
	26.		Visited all Staff Captains. Inspected and saw O.Cs., Q.Ms. stores of 5th Notts & Derby Regt, 2/6 and 2/7 Notts & Derby Regts.	
	27/30.		Routine.	

J Dado
Capt
DADOS
59th Div

A5834 Wt. W4973/M687 750,000 8/16 D. D. & L. Ltd. Forms/C.2118/13.

Confidential

Dasos
59 on

Vol 16

WAR DIARY

from

1st May 1918 — 31st May 1918

Volume No 16.

Instructions regarding War Diaries and Intelligence Summaries are contained in F. S. Regs., Part II. and the Staff Manual respectively. Title Pages will be prepared in manuscript.

WAR DIARY
or
INTELLIGENCE SUMMARY
(Erase heading not required.)

Army Form C. 2118

Place	Date	Hour	Summary of Events and Information	Remarks and references to Appendices
	1918. MAY			
	1-3.		Routine.	
	4		Transferred Office and stores from BAMBECQUE to KRUYSTRAETE Map ref. W.20.C.6.3.,Sheet No.19.	
	5-6.		Routine.	
	7.		Transferred part of Office and stores from KRUYSTRAETE, Map ref. W.20.C.6.3., Sheet No.19 to Jute Factory, ST.OMER.	
	8.		Completed transfer of stores and Office from KRUYSTRAETE, Map ref. W.20.C.6.3.,Sheet No.19 to Jute Factory,ST.OMER. All Infantry Battns, M.G.Battns, and 6/7 Royal Scots Fusrs. returned Mob. equipment excepting transport. Work was commenced on 8th inst. the units bringing in and laying out the equipment where it was checked by a Warrant Officer and receipt given. All stores were then packed in cases and sacks by the Ordnance Staff, sent to Railhead and loaded in trucks, detailed lists being made out in quadruplicate (3 for R.O.O. and one as my receipt). Serviceable and unserviceable stores were sent separately, and nine ten ton trucks were required (Winter clothing and blankets had previously been disposed of). All Machine Guns were returned to No.2 Gun Park, 10 three ton lorry loads being used. The actual work took 45 men 30 actual working hours and the amount of stores handled is estimated at 150 tons.	
	9-10.		Routine.	
	11.		Transferred office and stores from Jute Factory,ST.OMER to DIEVAL, Map ref. O.7.Cent. Sheet 36B.	
	12-16.		Routine.	
	17.		A.D.O.S., 10th Corps called.	
	18.		Visited Staff Captains 176, 177, and 178 Infantry Brigades.	
	19-21.		Routine.	
	22.		Visited A.D.O.S., 10th Corps.	
	23.		Visited Staff Captains 177 and 1 78th Infy. Bdes.	
	24-27.		Routine.	
	28.		Visited Staff Captain 176th Infantry Brigade.	
	29-30.		Routine.	
	31.		A.D.O.S., 10th. Corps called.	

S Dodd Capt
DADOS
59th Div

1875 Wt. W593/826 1,000,000 4/15 J.B.C. & A. · A.D.S.S./Forms/C. 2118.

Army Form C. 2118.

DADOS 59 D

Vol 17

WAR DIARY
or
INTELLIGENCE SUMMARY.
(Erase heading not required.)

Instructions regarding War Diaries and Intelligence Summaries are contained in F. S. Regs., Part II. and the Staff Manual respectively. Title pages will be prepared in manuscript.

Place	Date	Hour	Summary of Events and Information	Remarks and references to Appendices
	1918.			
JUNE	1.		Routine.	
	2.		D.D.O.S.,1st Army and A.D.O.S., 10th Corps called and inspected Office and stores.	
	3.		Visited Staff Captain 176th InfyBrigade.	
	4.		Routine.	
	5.		Visited Staff Captain 178th Infantry Brigade.	
	6/7.		Routine.	
	8.		Visited Staff Captain 177th Infantry Brigade.	
	9.		Routine.	
	10.		Visited A.D.O.S., 10th Corps.	
	10/12.		Visited Ordnance Depot, CALAIS, spent a day in a Group, Issues Branch &c. and part of a day going over the Salvage at VENDROUX.	
	12.		Returned from Ordnance Depot, CALAIS.	
	13/16.		Routine.	
	17.		A.D.O.S., 10th Corps called. Transferred Office and stores from DIEVAL to CREPY.	
	18/19.		Routine.	
	20.		Visited Os.C. all Infantry Battns, and Staff Captains 176th, 177th 178th Infantry Brigades .	
	22/24.		Routine.	
	25.		Capt.J.DODDS appointed to rank of T/Major whilst holding appointment of D.A.D.O.S., as from 25th Feby.1918.	
	26/30.		Routine.	

J Dodds
Major.
D.A.D.O.S., 59th Division.

A5834 Wt. W4973/M687 750,000 8/16 D. D. & L. Ltd. Forms/C.2118/13.

Instructions regarding War Diaries and Intelligence Summaries are contained in F. S. Regs., Part II. and the Staff Manual respectively. Title Pages will be prepared in manuscript.

Army Form C. 2118

WAR DIARY
or
INTELLIGENCE SUMMARY
(Erase heading not required.)

DADOS 59 D

Vol 18

Place	Date	Hour	Summary of Events and Information	Remarks and references to Appendices
1918. JULY	1-5.		Routine.	
	6.		A.D.O.S., Canadian Corps called and inspected stores.	
	7.		Visited A.D.O.S., Canadian Corps.	
	8-24.		Routine.	
	25.		Transferred Office and Stores from CREPY to GOUY-EN-ARTOIS.	
	26.		Routine.	
	27.		Visited A.D.O.S., 6th Corps.	
	28.		Visited Ordnance Gun Park No.3.	
			Major J,DODDS, D.A.D.O.S., granted Special leave to England from this date, No.S/5098, Condr, S.E.RICHARDSON acting as DADOS, during the period of Major DODDS' absence. ADOS, VI Corps called and inspected Stores.	
	29-31.		Routine.	

J Dodds

Major.
D.A.D.O.S., 59th Division.

1875 Wt. W593/826 1,000,000 4/15 J.B.C. & A. A.D.S.S./Forms/C. 2118.

<u>Confidential.</u>

Vol 19

War Diary

of

DADOS 59th Division

From 1st Aug: 1918

To 31st Aug 1918

Volume No 19

Instructions regarding War Diaries and Intelligence Summaries are contained in F. S. Regs., Part II. and the Staff Manual respectively. Title Pages will be prepared in manuscript.

WAR DIARY
or
INTELLIGENCE SUMMARY
(Erase heading not required.)

Army Form C. 2118

Place	Date	Hour	Summary of Events and Information	Remarks and references to Appendices
1918.				
AUG.	1-3.		Routine.	
	4.		A.D.O.S., VIth Corps called and inspected Office and stores.	
	5-7.		Routine.	
	8.		A.D.O.S., VIth Corps called.	
	9-10.		Routine.	
	11.		A.D.O.S., VI Corps called and inspected Office and stores.	
	12.		Major J. DODDS, (DADOS) returned off Special leave to England.	
	13-24.		Routine.	
	25.		Left GOUY EN ARTOIS for LA GOULEE, Map ref. N.30.D.3.8. Sht. 36A.	
	26.		A.D.O.S., XI Corps called.	
	27.		Visited A.D.O.S., XI Corps.	
			Transferred Office and stores from LA GOULEE Map ref. N.30.D.3.8. Sht. 36A to BUSNES.	
	28.		Routine.	
	29.		D.D.O.S., 5th Army called and inspected Office and stores.	
	30-31.		Routine.	

J. Dodds

Major.
DADOS, 59th Division.

1875 Wt. W593/826 1,000,000 4/15 J.B.C. & A. A.D.S.S./Forms/C. 2118.

CONFIDENTIAL. Vol 20

WAR DIARY
OF
D.A.D.O.S 59th DIVISION

FROM 1st SEPT 1918 TO 30th SEPT 1918

VOLUME. 20.

Instructions regarding War Diaries and Intelligence Summaries are contained in F. S. Regs., Part II. and the Staff Manual respectively. Title pages will be prepared in manuscript.

WAR DIARY
or
INTELLIGENCE SUMMARY.
(Erase heading not required.)

Army Form C. 2118.

Place	Date	Hour	Summary of Events and Information	Remarks and references to Appendices
	1918 SEPTEMBER			
	1-5		Routine.	
	6.		Transferred Stores from BUSNES to BEAUPRE Map.ref.L.32.C.9.8. Sheet No.36A.	
			A.D.O.S., XIth Corps called.	
	7.		Transferred Office from BUSNES to BEAUPRE Map ref.L.32.C.9.8. Sheet No.36A.	
	8-9.		Routine.	
	10.		A.D.O.S., XIth Corps called and inspected stores.	
	11-12.		Routine.	
	13.		Capt. C.C.HILLERY, A.I.F. attached as 'Q' Learner, reported and returned to Divl.Headquarters on completion.	
	14-18.		Routine.	
	19.		A.D.O.S., XIth Corps called and inspected stores.	
			Attended Conference of Staff Officers at Divl.Headquarters.	
	20-21.		Routine.	
	22.		A.D.O.S., XIth Corps, D.D.O.S.,5th Army,and Col.K.S.DUNSTERVILLE,CB. of War Office, LONDON called and inspected stores.	
			Capt. W.KIRTON,DCM.D.C.L.I., Attd. A.O.D. reported for instructional Course.	
	23.		Routine.	
	24.		A.D.O.S., XIth Corps called.	
	25.		Routine.	
	26.		Capt. W.KIRTON,DCM, D.C.L.I., Attd.A.O.D. completed instructional course and proceeded to 11th Corps Troops for duty.	
	~~27-30~~.		Attended Conference of Quartermasters at Divl. Headquarters.	
	27-30.		Routine.	

Major.
D.A.D.O.S., 59th Division.

A5834 Wt. W4973/M687 750,000 8/16 D. D. & L. Ltd. Forms/C.2118/13.

Confidential

Vol. 21

War Diary

of

D.A.D.O.S 59 Division

From 1st October 1918

To 31st October 1918.

Volume No. 22

Instructions regarding War Diaries and Intelligence Summaries are contained in F. S. Regs., Part II. and the Staff Manual respectively. Title pages will be prepared in manuscript.

WAR DIARY
or
INTELLIGENCE SUMMARY.

(Erase heading not required.)

Army Form C. 2118.

Place	Date	Hour	Summary of Events and Information	Remarks and references to Appendices
1918. OCTOBER	1-3.		Routine.	
	4.		A.D.O.S., XIth Corps called.	
			Transferred Office and stores from BEAUPRE to L.22.c.2.8.Sht.36A.	
	5-9.		Routine.	
	10.		Transferred Office and stores from L.22.c.2.8.Sht.36A to LAVENTIE.	
	11-15.		Routine.	
	16.		A.D.O.S., XIth Corps called.	
	17-20.		Routine.	
	21.		Transferred Office and part of stores from LAVENTIE to HEM.	
	22.		Continued transferred of stores from LAVENTIE to HEM.	
	23.		Completed transfer of stores from LAVENTIE to HEM.	
	24-31.		Routine.	

[signature]

Major.
D.A.D.O.S., 59th Division.

A5834 Wt. W4973/M687 750,000 8/16 D. D. & L. Ltd. Forms/C.2118/13.

Instructions regarding War Diaries and Intelligence Summaries are contained in F. S. Regs., Part II. and the Staff Manual respectively. Title pages will be prepared in manuscript.

WAR DIARY
or
INTELLIGENCE SUMMARY.
(Erase heading not required.)

Army Form C. 2118.

DADOS 59 Div
V8 22

Place	Date	Hour	Summary of Events and Information	Remarks and references to Appendices
	Nov.	1.2.	Routine.	
		3.	Visited A.D.O.S. 11th. Corps.	
		4.8.	Routine.	
		9.	A.D.O.S. 11th. Corps called.	
		10.	Routine.	
		11.	Transferred Office and Store from HEM to TEMPLEUVE	
		12.	Routine.	
		13.	Major J. Dodds proceeded to vl. Corps for Temporary duty.	
		14.15.	Routine.	
		16.	Capt. C.W.Bacon A.O.D. reported for temporary duty as D.A.D.O.S. Transferred Office and dump from TEMPLEUVE to WATTIGNIES.	
		17.	Routine.	
		18.	Called on A.D.O.S. who was out. Visited Divisional Laundry., found the place generally untidy. Brigades holding stocks of clothing which should be kept by Laundry- Instructed Corporal Moore, the N.C.O. in charge, to adjust it.	
		19.	Routine Office work. "Q" unable to give me a car.	

A5834 Wt. W4973/M687 750,000 8/16 D. D. & L. Ltd. Forms/C.2118/13.

Instructions regarding War Diaries and Intelligence Summaries are contained in F. S. Regs., Part II. and the Staff Manual respectively. Title pages will be prepared in manuscript.

WAR DIARY
or
INTELLIGENCE SUMMARY.

(Erase heading not required.)

Army Form C. 2118.

Place	Date	Hour	Summary of Events and Information	Remarks and references to Appendices
	Nov.	20.	Routine Office work in morning. Called on A.D.O.S. re the following subjects:- Stores held by Units under Mob. Store Tables - not required -. He agreed that such stores could be returned if Units desired and receipt given them by me (D.A.D.O.S.) . He spoke to D.D.O.S. Army on this subject who also agreed. The question of the return of Lewis Guns for Anti-Aircraft work is being taken up. Divisional Laundry: Corps Order No. 712, stated D.A.D.O.S. should be responsible for issueing and receipt of underclothing. A.D.O.S. explained that D.A.D.O.S. was only responsible for the ~~unopened numbers and~~ proper running and accounting of the Laundry. The Division should supply an Officer and the personnel.	
		21.	Office Routine. No cars available for D.A.D.O.S.	
		23.	Visited 176 and 178 Brigades. Both Staff Captains out. Office Routine in afternoon.	
		22.	Spoke to "Q" re Units returning Mob. Stores not required. "Q" are rather against this as they say such stores might be rquired in open warfare. They promised to let me have certificates from Brigades that all Units were up to Mob. Store Tables.	
		24.	Office Routine. No car available.	
		25.	Office Routine in morning. The Division is under orders to move to an area near NOEUX LES MINES. Visited 178 Brigade in afternoon. Staff Captain again out.	
		26.	Visited 36th. Northumberland Fusiliers and Officers Clothing Depot No. 5. N.C.O. in charge of Depot. said supply of Officers clothing was very low but authority had been obtained for increase of stocks. When this stock arrives there should be no need for D.A.D.O.S. to supply Officers with clothing on payment. Office Routine in afternoon.	
		27.	Visited new area with the D.A.A.G. A good site has been chosen for me at VENQUIN. D.H.Q. to be in Chateau at VAUDRICOURT.	

A5834 Wt. W4973/M687 750,000 8/16 D. D. & L. Ltd. Forms/C.2118/13.

Instructions regarding War Diaries and Intelligence Summaries are contained in F. S. Regs., Part II. and the Staff Manual respectively. Title pages will be prepared in manuscript.

WAR DIARY
or
~~INTELLIGENCE SUMMARY.~~
(Erase heading not required.)

Army Form C. 2118.

Place	Date	Hour	Summary of Events and Information	Remarks and references to Appendices
	Nov. 28.		Office Routine.	
	29.		Visited 5th. Army Headquarters and learn we are now under 1st. Army. Visited railhead and went to see A.D.O.S. X1. Corps., found he had moved to new area. I wanted a car all day but had to come back to lunch to find out if I could keep it for afternoon. On p'honing the D.A.Q.M.G. he tells me that I am not "playing the game" with the cars as I had kept the car in my dump instead of sending it back to the garage and that I could not have the car for the afternoon. The question of a car for D.A.D.O.S. gets worse. Spoke to the A.A. & Q.M.G. and told him I was not able to carry out my work unless I had a car more often. He said he would speak to the D.A.Q.M.G. and arrange it.	
	30.		Went to see A.D.O.S. X1. Corps at his new place - LA BUISSIERE. Found he was on leave. The acting A.D.O.S. was O.O. X1. Corps Troops, who was still at LE MADELAINE. Visited my new site with my Chief Clerk and allotted offices and dumps etc.	

[signature]
Capt.
A/D.A.D.O.S., 59th. Division.

A5834 Wt. W4973/M687 750,000 8/16 D. D. & L. Ltd. Forms/C.2118/13.

Instructions regarding War Diaries and Intelligence Summaries are contained in F. S. Regs., Part II. and the Staff Manual respectively. Title pages will be prepared in manuscript.

WAR DIARY
or
INTELLIGENCE SUMMARY.
(Erase heading not required.)

Army Form C. 2118.

DADOS 59 D
Vol 23

Place	Date	Hour	Summary of Events and Information	Remarks and references to Appendices
	1918			
DECR.	1.		Office routine. Q unable to give me a car although I told them I requir ed one urgently on account of the move. The move to take please on the forth instant.	
	2.		Office reutine. No car available. Apply to Q for a car for three days during move. The move is now to take place on the 6th The 178th Infantry Brigade is under orders to proceed to DUNKERQUE.	
	3.		Office routine. The DAQMG (Major BRADSTOCK) and Capt. DIMOCK visited me as regards my application for a car for three days during move, and stated that this was not possible. I pointed out the fact that DADOS was allowed a car by War Establishment (1918). Major BRADSTOCK said that this was cancelled as all cars had to be pooled He would do what he could for me, although I had had a car far more often than Major DODDS (late DADOS) ever had.	
	4.		Office routine. Went to Base Cashier, LILLE. Two lorries clear Railhead and go direct to new dump at VERQUIN, and the other two lorries move part of dump to VERQUIN with Cobdr. RIVHARDSON, and Sub.Condr. VALENTINE.. Condr. RICHARDSON returned with three lorries in evening and reports that CRE has occupied the best sheds in the site allotted to me, also the Divisional Laundry was occupying three stables. Go and see Q, who states that the DAAG (Major SCOTT MURRAY) is at VAUDRICOURT who is doing the allotting of sites. The AA &QMG (col. WESTLEY) says CRE will have to clear out if I have not room.	
	5.		Remainder of dump and personnel moved to VERQUIN. Closed Office at WATTIGNIES at11.15 a.m. After much difficulty Q find me a seat in the Signals car to take me to VERQUIN. Arrive VERQUIN 1600 hours. and find CRE and Laundry well established in my site. Phone Major SCOTT MURRAY who promises to come round and see me in morning.	
	6.		Capt. DIMOCK comes to see me as regards the site, as the DAAG has gome to GERMANY. Promises to speak to AA & QMG. The AA & QMG comes to see me and I inform him that either the CRE or myself must clear out of this site, as it is not large enough for us both.	

A5834 Wt. W4973/M687 750,000 8/16 D. D. & L. Ltd. Forms/C.2118/13.

Army Form C. 2118.

Instructions regarding War Diaries and Intelligence Summaries are contained in F. S. Regs., Part II. and the Staff Manual respectively. Title pages will be prepared in manuscript.

WAR DIARY
or
INTELLIGENCE SUMMARY.
(Erase heading not required.)

Place	Date	Hour	Summary of Events and Information	Remarks and references to Appendices
	6.		Sheet No.2.	
			Met CRE who states that Q have agreed to his remaining in the site, but the Laundry is to go.	
			The move of 178th Infantry Brigade is cancelled.	
	7/8		Office routine.	
	9.		Visited Railhead NOEUX LES MINES, 2/6 Durham L.I. and 15th Bn.Essex Rgt. These two Battns. find it difficult to keep within the ration of SD. Clothing. Called on Staff Captain 177th Bde. who was out, and Staff Captain 176th Infy. Bde. Tried to get to No.1 Ordce. Gun Park at SOMAINES but owing to bad roads did not get further than DOUAI.	
			178th Infy. Bde now ordered to move to DUNKERQUE on 10th.	
	10		The AA & QMG sends for me, and wants to know why I took the car to DOUAI yesterday. He thinks I should not go on these long distances without telling him. I told him I thought if a DADOS was allotted a car for the day, surely he knew which were the most important places to visit.	
			Attended Conference at DHQ. re the men's Xmas. dinner. The Divisional Canteen is going to give 2 franss per head towards the dinner.	
			Office routine in afternoon. 178th Infy. Bde. leave for DUNKERQUE.	
	11.		Office routine in morning. Called on ADOS, 11th Corps for a ruling as to whether I should send a Brigade Ordnance staff with 178th Infy. Bde. in view of their going on to the L.of C He phones Army who states Bde. Staff must accompany the Brigade.	
			ADOS instructs me to wear the blue gorget patches and cap band. On my return I inform the DAQMG of the ADOS instructions, but he does not agree and wants me to refer the matter to ADOS again.	
	12.		Office routine. CRE clears out of my site.	
	13.		Office routine. I wanted to visit No.1 Ordce. Gun Park at SOMAINES on the question of transfer to base of the supply of guns, but am unable to do so, as Q are unable to spare a car for these long journeys!	
			Laundry leaves my site.	
	14.		Office routine in morning. Sent one lorry to DUNKERQUE with Bde.Ordce.	

A5834 Wt. W4973/M687 750,000 8/16 D. D. & L. Ltd. Forms/C.2118/13.

WAR DIARY
or
INTELLIGENCE SUMMARY.
(*Erase heading not required.*)

Instructions regarding War Diaries and Intelligence Summaries are contained in F. S. Regs., Part II. and the Staff Manual respectively. Title pages will be prepared in manuscript.

Army Form C. 2118.

Sheet 3

Place	Date	Hour	Summary of Events and Information	Remarks and references to Appendices
Dec.	15		Routine.	
	16.		Routine - Bulk demands of 28/11 & 4/12 for 838 prs of Boots had not been met by 16/12 so Army authy. was ~~[illegible]~~ wired for to send lorry to Calais to fetch them. All units badly needed boots.	
	17.		Routine - Lorry left for Calais for Boots.	
	18.		Routine - Lorry returned from Calais with 469 prs of boots of demand dt. 12/12. Calais stated that ~~[illegible]~~ the demands of Bulk indents dt. 28/11 & 4/12 had been despatched by train.	
	19.		Routine - The train with boots arrived - but only contained 131 prs of Boots. The sending of lorry to Calais has saved the situation for the moment - especially with the short issue on the train. Labour & P of W Coys. come under my administration. Wrote A.D.O.S. as to whether they come under G.R.O. 4773 for the rationing of clothing - as they are entitled to two suits per man.	
	20		The AA & QMG phoned & said I had not visited the 277 A.F.A Bde - and they badly wanted Ordnance Stores. Replied that I was visiting the Artillery today - as I had been promised a car. and that I should have done so before if a car had been available. — This is the first car allotted to me for 8 days. Visited Div. Arty. and 277 A.F.A Bde. The O.C. A.F.A Bde thought he had arranged with the AA & QMG for me to go out tomorrow - as he had wanted to get statements & indents in from his Batteries. Promised to go out next morning. ~~[illegible]~~ Called on A.D.O.S. XI Corps & discussed the question of rationing of clothing for units with authority for two suits per man. A.D.O.S. [illegible]	[illegible initials]

A5834 Wt. W4973/M687 750,000 8/16 D. D. & L. Ltd. Forms/C.2118/13.

Instructions regarding War Diaries and Intelligence Summaries are contained in F. S. Regs., Part II and the Staff Manual respectively. Title Pages will be prepared in manuscript.

WAR DIARY
or
INTELLIGENCE SUMMARY
(Erase heading not required.)

Army Form C. 2118

Sheet 4

Place	Date	Hour	Summary of Events and Information	Remarks and references to Appendices
Decr	20	(cont)	that each case must be decided on its merits - bearing in mind the rationing scheme.	
	21.		Could not get car in morning - but did so in afternoon. Went to the 277 A.F.A. Bde & found the O.C. had gone out, as he had given me up - as he had not got my message that I could not get a car for the morning. Went through Indents with the Adjutant. This Bde has not had any Ordnance Stores for some months, owing to ~~moving~~ continually moving about. ~~this~~ They had never drawn any Horse Rugs. On my return, arranged to issue some of the stores due to other units - so as to assist this Bde, as they are far worse off than any other unit in the Division.	
	22		Routine -	
	23.		Routine + - Artillery G.O.C. (Brigadier General James) called to know how I was getting on. Small units continue to come under my administration - and want boots & remaining material. Cannot do much for them as luckily the 277 A.F.A. Bde - makes units in the Division cannot be notified of any more boots.	
	24.		Routine. A letter is received from H.Q. that Major Dodds is to be appointed A.D.O.S. XI Corps & will not return to this Div.	
	25		Routine. Closed down at 13.00 hrs. The men have their Xmas dinner at [illegible] 17.00 hrs.	
	26		Routine. Pt McCarthy R.A.O.C. is evacuated with strained ankle.	
	27.		Routine. The position of Boots ~~& leather~~ gets worse - as no leather soles have been received since 14/12. Spent today in bed, as I have wrenched one of my bad wrists.	
	28.		Routine. 860 prs of Boots received by means of my demand for 1135 prs. Also a supply of leather Soles.	
	29.		Routine. Visit A.D.O.S. XI Corps - on general matters. He informs me, as far he knows, that I shall be appointed D.A.D.O.S. to the Division. - 176 Infy Bde. ordered to move to	

1875 Wt. W593/826 1,000,000 4/15 J.B.C. & A. A.D.S.S./Forms/C. 2118.

Instructions regarding War Diaries and Intelligence Summaries are contained in F. S. Regs., Part II. and the Staff Manual respectively. Title pages will be prepared in manuscript.

WAR DIARY
or
INTELLIGENCE SUMMARY.
(Erase heading not required.)

Army Form C. 2118.

Sheet 5.

Place	Date	Hour	Summary of Events and Information	Remarks and references to Appendices
Deu[illegible]	29 (Contd)		to XIX Corps for forming demobilisation Camp. Obtained car in afternoon & visited 176 Bde ~~on the gas~~ & the Welsh Fusiliers on the question of Boots. The Welsh Fusiliers said they were alright - now that they had got an issue today. Thought the remaining material had arrived too late. Staff Capt 176 Bde - wishes me to make sure the issue of boots done - ~~[illegible]~~ Returned to Office & wired Army for authority to send lorry to Calais for Boots. Got another car and went & saw the Corps. They badly wanted boots - arranged to issue directly lorry returned from Calais. Again visited Staff Capt 176 Bde: told him what was arranged.	
	30.		Routine. - Lorries left for Calais.	
	31.		Move of Sussex, [illegible] and Field ambulance cancelled for present. Visited Sussex & told them owing to ~~[illegible]~~ the cancellation of move - I would not issue boots until the next day and that they should commence repairing boots. Lorry returned with 504 prs of boots.	

[signature] Capt.
A/D.A.D.O.S.
59 Division

A5834 Wt. W4973/M687 750,000 8/16 D. D. & L. Ltd. Forms/C.2118/13.

Instructions regarding War Diaries and Intelligence Summaries are contained in F. S. Regs., Part II. and the Staff Manual respectively. Title Pages will be prepared in manuscript.

WAR DIARY
or
INTELLIGENCE SUMMARY
(Erase heading not required.)

DADOS 59 Div

Vol 24

59

Army Form C. 2118

Place	Date	Hour	Summary of Events and Information	Remarks and references to Appendices
1919 Jany	1		Visited 23rd Labour Group who stated that the Labour Coys joining him are all in a very bad way for Clothing, Boots &c Visited 735 Labour Coy and 121 Ch.L.C. with the Adjt of the Gp. I found the Labour Gp. quite correct The 735 Labour Coy had 30 men who could not leave Camp for want of Clothing, and 82 Chinks of the 121 C.L. Coy had refused to work for want of boots. I went to ADOS Corps and got him to wire 1st Army for authy to send lorries to Calais for 1000 prs boots 1000 half soles 200 sets SD Clothing and Chinese Clothing	
	2		Office Routine. 1st Army authy recd. in evening for lorry to proceed to Calais for boots &c for Labour Gp, 1st Army wants full report on condition of Labour Coys	
	3		Lorries left for Calais. Visited the 25 L'pool Regt who are fairly well off for boots. Also visited the 17th R Sussex Regt. to find out the exact No. of they required for their move, and investigated why they had not indented for more boots as they were well under their ration. Also visited 277 AFA Bde they are badly in want of Horse Rugs.	

1875 Wt. W593/826 1,000,000 4/15 J.B.C. & A. A.D.S.S./Forms/C. 2118.

Instructions regarding War Diaries and Intelligence Summaries are contained in F. S. Regs., Part II. and the Staff Manual respectively. Title pages will be prepared in manuscript.

WAR DIARY
or
INTELLIGENCE SUMMARY.
(Erase heading not required.)

Army Form C. 2118.

Place	Date	Hour	Summary of Events and Information	Remarks and references to Appendices
Jany	4		The 17 R Sussex Regt leave for HODINGHEM Hastened Base for Horse Rugs. for 277 Bde AFA. Visited 277 Bde AFA and 25 L'pool Regt.	
	5		Office Routine	
	6.		-do- Closed Office and Stores at 1300 hours.	
	7.		HQ Fd. Coy RE. left for DUNKIRK. Transferred to COO Dunkirk for Ordce. The situation of boots and nose bags still very bad. Wired for Army Authy to send lorry to Calais for some.	
	8		Office Routine.	
	9.		Visited ADOS Corps and 1/3 NM. Fd ambce. Lorry went to Calais to get boots &c. Condr Richardson proceeded on Special Leave	
	10/11		Office Routine.	
	12		-do- 177 Inf Bde ordered to move to L of C.	
	13.		HQ 177 Infy Bde 11 Lon L. 177 L T M Btty 3 Sect Sig Coy RE. leave for Abancourt 1 Coy of HLI to Abbeville	
	14		Office Routine. 11 Corps order order three of my lorries to be withdrawn Wrote Q explaining necessity of retaining them. Spoke to ADOS about this. 15 Sussex Regt left for Dieppe.	[initials]

A5834 Wt. W4973/M687 750,000 8/16 D. D. & L. Ltd. Forms/C.2118/13

Army Form C. 2118.

Instructions regarding War Diaries and Intelligence Summaries are contained in F. S. Regs., Part II. and the Staff Manual respectively. Title pages will be prepared in manuscript.

WAR DIARY
or
INTELLIGENCE SUMMARY.
(Erase heading not required.)

Place	Date	Hour	Summary of Events and Information	Remarks and references to Appendices
Jan	14		7/6 Durham L.I. left for Dieppe. This completes move of 177 Inf Bde	
	15		25 L'pool Regt left for Walla Capelle to rejoin 176 Bde. 11 Corps auth: lorries to be retained today, so as to get stores to Barlin and Olhain for the formation of Animal Collecting & Staging Camps.	
			a/Sub/Cdr Greenland reported for duty as BWO 176 Inf Bde	
	16		Attended G.O.C. Conference at D.H.Q. 3 lorries returned to ~~[illegible]~~ Unit.	
	17		Office Routine. First Army auth: the Bde Ordce Staff of the 177 Bde to remain with me. But Bde Ord Staff of 176 Bde have to go 16	
	~~18~~		19 Corps Tps for the administering of the Bde	
	18/20		Office Routine	
	21		Went round the country trying to purchase leather for repairing boots. The only place I could find any was at St Pol. The price of this was 28 frs per Kilo. The DAQMG spoke to me about complaints O.C's had made to G.O.C at a recent meeting, that they were being issued with dirty and oiled stained clothing, also that the Ration was not sufficient. I told the DAQMG that only new S.D. Clothing was being issued, but would have every suit examined before issue for a	

A5834 Wt. W4973/M687 750,000 8/16 D. D. & L. Ltd. Forms/C.2118/13.

Instructions regarding War Diaries and Intelligence Summaries are contained in F. S. Regs., Part II. and the Staff Manual respectively. Title pages will be prepared in manuscript.

WAR DIARY
or
INTELLIGENCE SUMMARY.
(Erase heading not required.)

Army Form C. 2118.

Place	Date	Hour	Summary of Events and Information	Remarks and references to Appendices
	21		period of a week. The question of an excess issue of clothing was entirely a matter for the OC of the Unit. The DADMS wants to move the Laundry to Vandricourt or Verquin so that I can keep ~~in~~ ~~[illegible]~~ in closer touch with it. Promised to try and find a site for it. The running of the Laundry is a Q ~~matter~~ DADOS being only responsible for the accounting. I wrote ADOS Corps that I am willing to serve on with the BEF providing I am employed in the rank of major.	
	22		Office Routine	
	23		– do – Spent the afternoon in walking to Nœux les Mines to 2/3 NM Fd Ambce	
	24		Visited 25 KRRC. The men are well equipped for the move. Also visited 295 Bde RFA Bde Ord Staff for 176 Inf Bde left for 19 Corps Tps No 1	
	25		The 25 KRRC leave for Dunkirk.	
	26		Routine	

A5834 Wt. W4973/M687 750,000 8/16 D. D. & L. Ltd. Forms/C.2118/13.

Army Form C. 2118.

Instructions regarding War Diaries and Intelligence Summaries are contained in F. S. Regs., Part II. and the Staff Manual respectively. Title pages will be prepared in manuscript.

WAR DIARY
or
INTELLIGENCE SUMMARY.
(Erase heading not required.)

Place	Date	Hour	Summary of Events and Information	Remarks and references to Appendices
Jany	27		Went to St Pol to buy leather - to meet urgent demands	
	28.		Major Braddock DADMS visited me and discussed the lorry question. Will try & get Corps to give me another lorry and meanwhile will arrange for the DAG to supply me with 4 GS wagons.	
	29		Office Routine - 4 GS Wagons report.	
	30		11 Corps authorises me to have 2 lorries on permanent detail & 1 to be held at Corps for me to draw on when necessary. 470 Fd Coy ordered to move to Etaples.	
	31.		470 Fd Coy leave for Etaples.	
			The great shortage of boot leather during the month has caused and increased issue in boots. Nos. being administered for Order Tps 22600 Horses 3000	
			[signature] Major DADOS 59 Division	

A5834 Wt. W4973/M687 750,000 8/16 D. D. & L. Ltd. Forms/C.2118/13.

O.S. 10/55

H.Q. 59 Division

Herewith my War Diary for December. Regret the delay and also that the last few pages are not typed.

[illegible] Capt
A/D.A.D.O.S.
59 Div

10/1/19

Instructions regarding War Diaries and Intelligence Summaries are contained in F. S. Regs., Part II. and the Staff Manual respectively. Title Pages will be prepared in manuscript.

WAR DIARY
or
INTELLIGENCE SUMMARY
(Erase heading not required.)

Army Form C. 2118.

DADOS

Vol: 25

Place	Date	Hour	Summary of Events and Information	Remarks and references to Appendices
1919 Feby	1		Visited ADOS 11th Corps re Miniature V.C. Ribbon for 2/Lt. JOHNSON 36th Bn Northum. Fusrs ~~Received~~ Divn under orders to proceed to L of C.	
	2-7		Routine.	
	8.		Visited ADOS 11th Corps to get Medal Ribbons and as regards miniature V.C for 2/Lt JOHNSON. ADOS unable to get miniature V.C without copy of Authy and has taken no action. On my return forwarded report to Q.	
	9-10.		Routine	
	11		Capt. C.W. BACON appointed DADOS, 59 Divn and to be acting Major as from 14th Novr 1918.	
	12.		Routine.	
	13.		Transferred all units other than Divl Units to other Ordce Formations as this Divn is under orders to go to L of C.	
	14		Routine.	
	15.		Visited 295 and 296 Bde R.F.A.	
	16		Routine.	

Army Form C. 2118.

Instructions regarding War Diaries and Intelligence Summaries are contained in F. S. Regs., Part II. and the Staff Manual respectively. Title Pages will be prepared in manuscript.

WAR DIARY
or
INTELLIGENCE SUMMARY

(Erase heading not required.)

Place	Date	Hour	Summary of Events and Information	Remarks and references to Appendices
1919 Feby	17		Thaw precautions came into force from 0100 hours. Opened store at BARLIN, and one for unserviceable stores to be returned to Salvage Dump BARLIN. Sent necessary staff.	
	18		Went to Barlin.	
	19-21		Routine	
	22		Visited BARLIN Dump & Railhead with Condr. RICHARDSON.	
	23		Routine.	
	24		Thaw precautions finished. Visited RTO re returning trucks to Base	
	25-27		Routine.	
	28		Major Bacon DADOS proceeded on Leave	

[illegible] Bacon Major
DADOS.

2449 Wt. W14957/M90 750,000 1/16 J.B.C. & A. Forms/C.2118/12.

Instructions regarding War Diaries and Intelligence Summaries are contained in F. S. Regs., Part II. and the Staff Manual respectively. Title Pages will be prepared in manuscript.

WAR DIARY
or
INTELLIGENCE SUMMARY
(Erase heading not required.)

D.A.D.O.S. NO. ... APR 1919 59TH. DIVISION

Vol 26

Army Form C. 2118

Place	Date	Hour	Summary of Events and Information	Remarks and references to Appendices
Verquin	1-3-19	-	Routine	
-"-	1-6	-	Routine	
	7	-	Warrant officer proceeded in advance to take over dump at Le Beau Marais	
Beau Marais	8	-	closed dump at Verquin + reopened at Le Beau Marais	
-"-	9	-	Visited COO Calais to arrange new system of drawing of stores etc	
-"-	10-14		Routine	
	15		Major Bacon D.A.D.O.S. returned from leave. Visit of D.D.O.S. N	
-"-	16		Routine	
	17		Visited COO. Calais	
	18		-"- Demob Depôt	
-"-	19		Routine	
	20		Visited COO MGRS ref furnishing of camp	
-"-	21		Visit of D.D.O.S. (N)	
-"-	22 to 25		Routine	
-"-	26		Visited Dunkirk 176 + 178 Bde Staff Captains at Dunkirk also O.C. 11 Royal Scots	
-"-	27		Routine	
	28		Visited COO Calais and O.C. 2/6 D.L.I.	
	29 to 31		Routine	

H Bacon Major
D.A.D.O.S. 59 Division

Instructions regarding War Diaries and Intelligence Summaries are contained in F. S. Regs., Part II. and the Staff Manual respectively. Title Pages will be prepared in manuscript.

12

WAR DIARY
or
~~INTELLIGENCE SUMMARY~~

(Erase heading not required.)

Army Form C. 2118

59

Vol 27

Place	Date	Hour	Summary of Events and Information	Remarks and references to Appendices
Dean Marais	April 19			
	1	–	Routine	
	2	–	Visited D.D.O.S. L of C N	
	3	–	Routine	
	4		Visited C.O.O. Calais	
	5 & 6		Routine	
	7		Visit of D.D.O.S. N who inspected system of working & all books	
	8 – 11		Routine	
	12		Inspected equipt of 2/3 F.A. who have been ordered to reduce to Cadre	
	13-14		Routine	
	15		Inspected equipt of 469 F. Coy who have been ordered to reduce to Cadre	
	16		Routine	
	17		Inspected equipt of 2/2 Fd Amb & 467 Fd Coy who have been ordered to reduce to Cadre	
	15-22		Routine	
	23		Inspected equipt of 2/1 M.V. Sec who have been ordered to reduce to Cadre	
	24 & 25		Visited C.O.O. Calais to arrange for immediate issue of all stores for the battalions of 176 Brigade i.e. 25th Bn King's Liverpool Regt, 17th Bn R Sussex & 26th Bn R Welsh Regt. All stores including ammunition issued to units in 36 hours.	
	26		Drill Khaki drawn & issued to units	
	27		Visited 177 Brigade	
	28		Routine	
	29		Routine	
	30		Visited 176 & 178 Brigades	

[illegible] 1st May 1919

A W Bacon
Major
D.A.D.O.S.
59 Division

1875 Wt. W593/826 1,000,000 4/15 J.B.C. & A. A.D.S.S./Forms/C. 2118.

Army Form C. 2118.

DADOS 59D

9/8 28

Instructions regarding War Diaries and Intelligence Summaries are contained in F. S. Regs., Part II. and the Staff Manual respectively. Title pages will be prepared in manuscript.

WAR DIARY
or
INTELLIGENCE SUMMARY.
(Erase heading not required.)

Place	Date	Hour	Summary of Events and Information	Remarks and references to Appendices
Beaumaris	1-7.		Routine.	
	8.		Visited 202. Field Coy.	
	9.		do. 2/3. Field ambulance	
	10-12.		Routine.	
	13.		Inspected equipment of 200, 202, 467, 470. Field Coys R.E. reduce to Cadre	
	14.		do do of 225. Field Coy. R.E. to reduce to Cadre	
	15.		Routine.	
	16.		Visited 177-178 Brigades & 2/2. Field ambulance	
	17-18.		Routine	
	19.		Interviewed 51. O.R. for attachment to R.A.O.C. under G.R.O. 6538.	
	20.		Routine.	
	21.		Visited 176. Brigade, 26. R. Welsh Fus, 13th West Riding Regt & 2/2 Field ambulance	
	22-25.		Routine	
	26.		Visited No. 274 Coy. A.S.C.	
	27-28.		Routine	
	29.		Visited 2/3 Field ambulance.	
	30.		do. 177. Brigade	
	31.		Routine	

[signature]
Major
DADOS 59 DW

D. D. & L., London, E.C.
(A10266) Wt W5300/P713 750,000 2/18 Sch. 52 Forms/C2118/16

Instructions regarding War Diaries and Intelligence Summaries are contained in F. S. Regs., Part II. and the Staff Manual respectively. Title pages will be prepared in manuscript.

WAR DIARY
or
INTELLIGENCE SUMMARY.
(*Erase heading not required.*)

Army Form C. 2118.

DADOS 59D

9/8/29

GENERAL STAFF No. G 1459 Date 2/7/19 59th (NORTH MIDLAND) DIVISION

Place	Date	Hour	Summary of Events and Information	Remarks and references to Appendices
BEAUMARAIS	2:6:19		Visited 177th Brigade	
	3:6:19		Visited 178th Inf. Brigade	
	5:6:19		Visited Cadre of 59th Divisional Artillery	
	9:6:19		Visited 2/6th Durham Light Infantry.	
	10:6:19		Visited 11th Somerset L.I. interviewing O.R.'s for attachment to R.A.O.C.	
	10:6:19		Visited 2/6th Durham L.I. interviewing O.R.'s for attachment to R.A.O.C.	
	~~11/6/19~~		~~:as on 10/6/19~~	
	17:6:19		Visited 176th Infantry Brigade and 178th Infantry Brigade.	
	24:6:19		Holiday granted on the occasion of Peace having been declared.	
	26:6:19		Visited C.O.O., Calais in reference to the suspension of issues of stores.	

[signature] Major
DADOS
59 Div

A6945 Wt. W11422/M1160 350,000 12/16 D. D. & L. Forms/C./2118/14.

DADOS 59 D

Army Form C. 2118.

Vol 30

Instructions regarding War Diaries and Intelligence Summaries are contained in F. S. Regs., Part II. and the Staff Manual respectively. Title pages will be prepared in manuscript.

WAR DIARY
or
INTELLIGENCE SUMMARY.
(Erase heading not required.)

Place	Date	Hour	Summary of Events and Information	Remarks and references to Appendices
Beaumarais - France	July.			
	1.		Visited 176 & 178 Infy.Bde., No.4 Coy.Train, & 2/3rd Field Ambulance.	
	2.		Major C.W.Bacon,O.B.E., D.A.D.O.S., proceeded on 14 days leave to U.K.	
	11.		Orders received for D.A.D.O.S. to close down & his staff to report to C.C.O.Calais for duty.	
	16.		Major C.W.Bacon,O.B.E.,D.A.D.O.S., returned off leave.	
	17.		Visited C.O.O.,Calais re.transfer of administration of Ordnance Services and found stores would take 7 weeks to reach units at Dunkerque if sent by A.M.F.O.	
	18.		Routine.	
	19.		Holiday in celebration of Peace.	
	21.		Routine.	
	22.		Routine.	
	23.		Routine.	
	24.		Visited C.C.O.Calais with the A.A.& Q.M.G. on question of stores taking 7 weeks to get to Dunkerque. It was arranged that stores for units at Dunkerque should be collected by Div.lorry direct from Vendroux Depot pending an improvement in the A.M.F.O.service.	
			Visited No.2?3 Coy.,59 Div: Train & carried out inspection of reduction to Cadre.	
	25.		Visited 178 Bde. & 176 L.T.B. and carried out inspection on reduction to Cadre.Visited C.C.O.Hoymille.	
	26.		Administration of the Div:for Ordnance services taken over by C.C.O.Calais. Visit C.O.O.Calais and arranged that I should remain here Monday & report to him on Tuesday.	
	28.		Condr.Richardson leaves for duty with O.C.,No.3 Area Laundry,Hesdigneul. ~~Finally closed office & stores. Leave with staff for duty with C.C.O.,Calais.~~	

C.W. Bacon Major,
D.A.D.O.S.
59th DIVISION.

A6945 Wt. W11422/M1160 350,000 12/16 D. D. & L. Forms/C./2118/14.

Instructions regarding War Diaries and Intelligence Summaries are contained in F. S. Regs., Part II. and the Staff Manual respectively. Title Pages will be prepared in manuscript.

WAR DIARY
or
INTELLIGENCE SUMMARY
(Erase heading not required.)

Army Form C. 2118

Place	Date	Hour	Summary of Events and Information	Remarks and references to Appendices
	July 28.		Orders received from D.D.O.S.(N). that I am not to leave the Division until everything is cleared up. A report to this effect is to be sent in before final departure.	
	29.		Routine.	
	30.		Routine.	
	31.		Visited 2/6th D.L.I. re. discrepancies. Also visited Ordnance Vendroux Depot and obtained G.S. Medal ribbon for the Division and Units.	

[signature]
Major,
D.A.D.O.S.,
59th Division.

1875 Wt. W593/826 1,000,000 4/15 J.B.C. & A. A.D.S.S./Forms/C. 2118.

www.ingramcontent.com/pod-product-compliance
Lightning Source LLC
Chambersburg PA
CBHW081432160426
43193CB00013B/2261